Cambridge Elements ☰

Elements in Music Since 1945
edited by
Mervyn Cooke
University of Nottingham

RHYTHM AND HERITAGE IN MODERN FLAMENCO GUITAR

Carlos van Tongeren
University of Manchester

CAMBRIDGE
UNIVERSITY PRESS

Shaftesbury Road, Cambridge CB2 8EA, United Kingdom

One Liberty Plaza, 20th Floor, New York, NY 10006, USA

477 Williamstown Road, Port Melbourne, VIC 3207, Australia

314–321, 3rd Floor, Plot 3, Splendor Forum, Jasola District Centre,
New Delhi – 110025, India

103 Penang Road, #05–06/07, Visioncrest Commercial, Singapore 238467

Cambridge University Press is part of Cambridge University Press & Assessment,
a department of the University of Cambridge.

We share the University's mission to contribute to society through the pursuit of
education, learning and research at the highest international levels of excellence.

www.cambridge.org
Information on this title: www.cambridge.org/9781009494540

DOI: 10.1017/9781009307925

When citing this work, please include a reference to the DOI 10.1017/9781009307925

First published 2025

A catalogue record for this publication is available from the British Library

ISBN 978-1-009-49454-0 Hardback
ISBN 978-1-009-30789-5 Paperback
ISSN 2632-7791 (online)
ISSN 2632-7783 (print)

Additional resources for this publication at www.cambridge.org/Tongeren

Cambridge University Press & Assessment has no responsibility for the persistence
or accuracy of URLs for external or third-party internet websites referred to in this
publication and does not guarantee that any content on such websites is, or will
remain, accurate or appropriate.

Rhythm and Heritage in Modern Flamenco Guitar

Elements in Music Since 1945

DOI: 10.1017/9781009307925
First published online: January 2025

Carlos van Tongeren
University of Manchester

Author for correspondence: Carlos van Tongeren,
carlos.vantongeren@manchester.ac.uk

Abstract: Discourses about rhythmic skill and feel have often been associated with forms of non-Western, and especially African and Afro-diasporic identity and heritage. How can we rethink rhythmic skill for the contemporary world where concepts of heritage and belonging are attaining new meanings across cultural and geographical borders? This Element addresses this question through the case study of modern flamenco guitar, an instrumental practice that has achieved daunting levels of rhythmic sophistication and has been flourishing across the globe for decades, even before flamenco was inscribed into UNESCO's list of Intangible Cultural Heritage in 2010. Drawing on examples from local guitar traditions in Jerez de la Frontera and Morón de la Frontera and from an online guitar contest launched during the Covid-19 pandemic, this Element explores how rhythm can shape new ways of understanding and performing heritage in the global and digital age.

Keywords: flamenco, guitar, rhythm, heritage, music

ISBNs: 9781009494540 (HB), 9781009307895 (PB), 9781009307925 (OC)
ISSNs: 2632-7791 (online), 2632-7783 (print)

Contents

1 Introduction

La bulería te mueve	*The bulería moves you*
A ti el soniquete te mueve	*Its soniquete moves you*
Si tú no tienes soniquete	*If you don't have soniquete*
Pa qué te metes	*Why would you get into it*

These are the lyrics from 'Soniquete', a composition by the world-renowned flamenco guitarist Paco de Lucía that is named after a term commonly used in flamenco parlance to define rhythmic 'air' or 'feel'. Soniquete moves you, sings the young vocalist Potito before the guitar comes in; but if you don't have it, you might better stay away. As Bernat Jiménez de Cisneros notes, these lyrics were meant to subtly mock the foreign audiences that de Lucía encountered on his international tours and who dared to clap along to his music despite being unfamiliar with the rhythms (2020, 323n35). As such, these lyrics illustrate what a traditionally localised genre like flamenco can do in international settings, not only for those who know it well but also for those who lack in-depth knowledge about flamenco but feel enthused nonetheless by its technical and rhythmic sophistication. In this Element, I will explore the musical and cultural work achieved by rhythm in increasingly transnational contexts of musical performance and pedagogy. Using modern flamenco guitar as a case study, I will start with the premise that concepts of rhythmic air, feel, and skill are dependent not only on a musician's ability to successfully navigate the metric structures and sedimented musical knowledge of a genre like flamenco but also on the broader discourses that envelop musical practice. In the context of flamenco, 'having' rhythm, as alluded to in 'Soniquete', is commonly seen as a sign not only of musical skill but also of a guitarist's successful participation in artistic and cultural identities, lineages, and affiliations. To examine the relation between rhythm and such broader cultural identifications in a systematic manner, I here propose to combine an analysis of rhythm in modern flamenco guitar with a critical discussion of musical heritage.

In recent years, heritage has become a highly visible concept in flamenco studies, especially since this music was inscribed into the list of Immaterial World Heritage by the United Nations Educational, Scientific and Cultural Organisation (UNESCO) in November 2010. To be sure, most scholarly responses to the recent 'heritagisation' of flamenco have been critical rather than positive. One of the main challenges highlighted by scholars is that bureaucracies of heritage management – represented, in the case of flamenco, by institutions such as Andalusia's regional government (Junta de Andalucía) and the European Union – tend to be more focused on advancing economic benefit than on stimulating social participation (Cruces Roldán, 2023, 268–269; Venegas, 2017, 223–226). Scholars have also raised concerns about the lack of improved socio-economic opportunities for the Spanish Roma, more commonly known as Gitanos.[1] While Gitanos were acknowledged in the UNESCO bid as crucial contributors to the development of flamenco, they have often not bene-fitted from funding allocations (Cruces Roldán, 2023, 279–281; Periáñez, 2019). Furthermore, prior to 2010, Andalusia's regional government had already attrib-uted itself 'the exclusive competency (*competencia*) in terms of knowledge, conservation, research, training, promotion and dissemination of flamenco as a singular element of Andalusian cultural heritage' (qtd. Cruces Roldán, 2023, 274) in its updated Statute of Autonomy from 2007. This claim, as José Luis Venegas has noted, leaves little room for grassroots communities in Andalusia and beyond to participate in the construction of flamenco as cultural heritage – let alone to interrogate what *inheriting* this music might actually mean (2017, 223–226).

In the context of this debate, the present study explores how rhythm is con-structed as cultural heritage through interrelated uses of musical discourse and practice. Firstly, I examine how artistic and pedagogical discourses about rhythm in flamenco guitar are structured around concepts of heritage – in other words, how discourses about rhythm in flamenco are also, to an extent, discourses about heritage. While existing flamenco scholarship tends to focus on institutionalised heritage discourses and agendas, I aim to show how, in the unofficial settings in which flamenco is commonly taught, performed, and discussed, heritage is part of a broader conceptual constellation where it interacts with cognate terms such as 'tradition', 'lineage', and 'ancestry'. Analysing such unofficial or, as I will name them, 'tactical' identifications with heritage helps me develop a better understand-ing of the artistic, cultural, and political implications of flamenco's associated discourses and imaginaries.

Secondly, I will explore how such identifications are established not only on a discursive level but also through practices of flamenco guitar. As Joshua Brown notes, flamenco is thoroughly shaped by 'notions of, including feelings and values connected to, local sites, settings and performance spaces in Andalusia' (2014, 9). Similarly, Matthew Machin-Autenrieth has examined how institutional measures to promote flamenco as cultural heritage have impacted on flamenco practices in the city of Granada. Based on local fieldwork among teachers and performers of flamenco guitar, Machin-Autenrieth observes that, when compar-ing notions of heritage in flamenco song and guitar, 'musical localism is more

---

[1] In this Element, I use the terms 'Spanish Roma' and 'Gitanos' interchangeably. I acknowledge that the term 'Gitanos' is more common in Spanish, but also wish to underscore that the word 'Roma' was adopted as the preferred endonym (instead of 'Gypsy') at the First World Romani Congress in London in 1971.

"tangible" when it comes to *cante*, remaining an allusive concept in guitar performance' (2017, 158). Contrary to this scholar's assessment, I will argue that rhythm, as practised in flamenco guitar, has strong and clear ties with concepts of cultural heritage. Highlighting such connections requires a theoretical framework that moves beyond the common notion that rhythm is an inherited musical skill – whether transmitted along racial or sociocultural lineages. Instead, I will argue that rhythm can bring about open-ended identifications with sedimented musical knowledge. Thus, I explore a semantics of rhythm that moves beyond notions of ownership and possession – which also underpins the concept of 'having rhythm' that I began with – towards a dynamic where rhythm partially resists inscriptions into recognisable lineages and identities. In this way, I argue, rhythm gestures towards emergent and open-ended concepts of heritage.

I hope that this new way of thinking about the dynamic between rhythm and heritage gives a stimulus to debates about the artistic, racial, and cultural lineages of rhythm spanning most of twentieth century; but also, that it enables new views about the transnational ramifications of a traditionally local genre like flamenco. As Ana María Ochoa noted over two decades ago, the relations between music and local territories are no longer self-evident as they are now negotiated in increasingly transnational contexts (2003, 46). This view certainly applies to the flamenco guitar, which, today, is at the heart of a global industry. Aspiring flamenco guitarists from virtually every corner of the world dedicate vast amounts of time, energy, and resources to travel to Spain and study with eminent maestros; international students spend hours per week on online platforms in search for useful guitar content to support their journeys of musical learning; flamenco guitar teachers, moreover, are offering lessons in virtually every mid-sized town across all continents; and guitar makers (*guitarreros*) are attracting growing numbers of tourists and buyers to their physical workplaces and web stores, thus contributing to the emergence of transnational 'guitar-scapes' (Dawe & Dawe, 2001). This broad variety of practices, pedagogies, and imaginaries around the flamenco guitar raises questions about the ways in which traditional flamenco discourse, structured around notions of purity, authenticity, and ancestral continuity, acquires new meanings for new audiences and practitioners beyond the local level. Indeed, if we aim for a truly global meaningfulness of flamenco *as* heritage – which appears to be what transnational heritage agendas envision – then careful attention needs to be paid to the ways in which modern practices of flamenco guitar overflow, and thus have the potential to challenge, traditional identifications with this music on a local level.

Throughout this Element, I will build on the work of various musicologists who have provided detailed classifications and analyses of the metrical structures of flamenco, known as *compases* (Jiménez de Cisneros, 2015; Sainz &

Mbengue, 2022), as well as of a variety of rhythmic phenomena such as embodied percussion, footwork, and *palmas* (handclapping) (De la Torre, 2019; Jiménez de Cisneros, 2020; Romero Naranjo, 2008). I will also engage with various non-academic sources about the flamenco guitar, such as analyses of the stylistic features of individual guitarists and local guitar traditions (among others, see Faucher, 1996; Worms, 2011). However, my analysis of rhythm and heritage in flamenco guitar is not strictly musicological and takes inspiration from a variety of other disciplinary fields, such as cultural studies, performance studies, and heritage studies. Thus, my exploration of rhythmic heritage dialogues with cultural analyses of the Afro-diasporic lineages of rhythm (Diouf & Kiddoe Nwankwo, 2010b; Feldman, 2006) and with a growing body of historically inflected scholarship that has examined the influence of Afro-diasporic traditions on flamenco (Castro, 2020; Goldberg, 2019; Núñez, 2021; Rodríguez, 2014). From the perspective of cultural studies and ethnography, my understanding of rhythm and heritage as interrelated musical and discursive categories builds on Lila Ellen Gray's study of Portuguese fado, which starts with the premise that the 'poetics about music making are inseparable from music's social life' (2013, 6), as well as on Kevin Dawe and Moira Dawe's suggestion that guitars, like other musical instruments, 'are empowered, not only by their sound but also by the written word, verbalizations, visual imagery, gestures and movements imbued with values and ideals that are created and maintained within specific social, cultural, political and economic settings' (2001, 64).

My analysis of modern flamenco guitar is interdisciplinary as well as practice-based. I have been a flamenco guitarist for over twenty years and have spent long periods in Andalusia, where I have studied and performed in a variety of formal and informal settings. My double background as a cultural scholar and flamenco musician has given me a keen interest not only in the intricacies of the rhythms of flamenco but also in the discourses that shape musical learning. Thus, the challenges and moments of musical fulfilment that I have experienced as a flamenco guitarist will be key points of reference here, as they have helped me navigate, and also challenge, ingrained perceptions about flamenco long before I started thinking about this study. Furthermore, my ways of observing and examining the embodied processes of flamenco guitar playing are informed by uncountable hours of guitar practice that have been a crucial part of my life for many years.

The argument of this Element is divided into four analytical sections and a conclusion. In Section 2, I build the theoretical framework for subsequent sections. I provide an overview of existing theoretical work on rhythm and heritage in a variety of contexts and discuss how rhythm operates at the intersection of musical discourse and practice. At the end of Section 2, I explore how rhythm builds on sedimented elements from the flamenco repertoire associated with a living past; but also, how it is a fluid and open-ended form of musical practice that has the capacity to resist identifications with pre-established frameworks of meaning. Thus, I theorise rhythm as a practice that hovers between identification and open-endedness and will suggest that this dynamic can also help us rethink concepts of musical heritage. Building on this framework, in Sections 3 and 4 I examine the intersections between rhythm and heritage in two local flamenco guitar traditions commonly associated with a distinctive type of rhythmic playing: Jerez de la Frontera (hereafter Jerez) and Morón de la Frontera (hereafter Morón). In these sections, I analyse historical discourses about rhythmic distinctiveness in both localities, as well as relevant features of the poetics, pedagogies, and musical practices of some of these traditions' most eminent representatives. In both sections, the tension between identification and open-endedness already alluded to informs my reading of rhythmic discourses and practices in Jerez and Morón, and here I will also interrogate my own ways of 'inscribing' rhythm into recognisable frameworks of meaning. Finally, Section 5 draws on examples from an online flamenco guitar contest launched during the Covid-19 pandemic to explore how contemporary rhythmic concepts are shaped by the new realities of a transnational and digitally mediated flamenco industry.

Throughout this Element, I will use the term 'modern' not as a reference to a rigid temporal framework, but rather in the way that this adjective is commonly used in flamenco parlance, where modern guitar practices are often counter-posed to more traditional ways of playing. The arrival of a modern style of flamenco guitar playing can broadly be attributed to the great advances in technical skill and harmonic and melodic richness made during the second half of the twentieth century. While eminent guitarists such as Niño Ricardo (1904–1972) and Sabicas (1912–1990) are among the first who initiated these developments, Paco de Lucía (1947–2014) is unanimously considered as the most revolutionary flamenco guitarist of all times.[2] For the purpose of this study, I will focus on developments in flamenco guitar in the wake of Paco de Lucía's ascension to fame in the late 1960s and early 1970s – especially after the release of his *rumba* 'Entre dos aguas' in 1973. Later generations of guitarists have largely built on the technical and compositional advances made by Paco de Lucía and his generational peers, such as Manolo Sanlúcar (1943–2022) and Serranito (1942–). On later pages, I will occasionally use the term 'contem-porary' when referring to some of these younger guitarists, such as Diego del

---

[2] For the sake of brevity and readability, in this Element I will identify all flamenco artists by using the artistic names under which they are commonly known.

Morao and Dani de Morón. My analysis of their work does not pretend to be exhaustive, and inevitably I will not be able to cover the contributions of some of these very influential guitarists with the attention each of them deserves. I hope, however, that this study will succeed in developing an analytical framework that can inform future critical work on the flamenco guitar.

A comment on translation seems in order. As this Element moves at the intersection of theoretical work, musical analysis, and cultural analysis, it dialogues with numerous publications and other sources in Spanish that have not been translated into English. All English translations of these sources are mine. Occasionally, when the original wording seemed particularly important, I have elected to print the original quotation alongside the English translation to allow the reader to capture the implication of certain terms, comments, or lyrics in the original language. Due to the brevity of this format, there is no scope for an exhaustive discussion of some of the terminology that I will employ throughout this Element. I offer brief working definitions of such terms when they first appear in the body of the text and have added a glossary as a separate document, where I expand slightly on relevant terms and signpost the reader to the work of other scholars who have discussed them in more detail. The reader is also invited to consult a Spotify playlist with an overview (where possible) of the compositions and recordings that I examine on later pages.[3]

The musical transcriptions that have been included in later sections were all created for this Element and have not been published elsewhere. While no single method for flamenco guitar notation exists to date, popular conventions in existing methods have been followed to convey some of the idiosyncrasies of flamenco guitar playing. Thus, taps on the guitar soundboard, known as *golpes*, are marked in the transcriptions with an asterisk.

2 Rhythm and Heritage

2.1 Rhythm, Metre, and Accentuation

In this Element, I broadly define rhythm as referring to the organisation of musical time. In the field of musicology, various theorists have observed how rhythm is reliant as much on structure as on a certain degree of irregularity. Pierre Sauvanet, for instance, defines rhythm as 'a fluid but constructed totality' ('un ensemble fluid mais construit') (2000, 144), a definition that encapsulates how rhythm is a way of ordering musical time that can also suggest tension, change, and movement. Roger Scruton's definition of rhythm points to the same

---

[3] The playlist is entitled 'Rhythm and Heritage in Modern Flamenco Guitar' and can be retrieved here: https://open.spotify.com/playlist/7qx81ufHfEPDgj2USobrMW?si=0991d50bba4b 43f5&pt=527dad6c1121e9ba17efe935159f6e12.

dynamic; he notes that '[r]hythm plays with regularity, but is not reducible to it: the pulse is both counted and discounted' (Scruton, 1997, 24). For Scruton, rhythm does not automatically result from the regular statement of the beat or pulse; rather, it emerges when musicians 'animate' the pulse by suggesting that beats bring each other into being instead of merely following one another (Scruton, 1997, 35). In a similar vein, the Spanish guitarist José María Gallardo observes that, in the context of flamenco, not playing the pulse can be a greater sign of rhythmic feel than performing it mechanically: '"[h]aving feel" or "playing with feel" isn't but [having] a pure and authentic understanding of rhythm in all its magnitude, without overemphasising the metric pulse, as the great majority of academically trained performers tend to do' (qtd. Torres Cortés, 2020, 143).

As can be seen, these scholars agree that rhythm reflects a musician's ability to creatively navigate an overarching temporal framework. Some theorists have indicated that rhythmic creativity is subject to a series of procedures that are musically and culturally specific. In other words, forms of rhythmic tension or discrepancy need to draw on a repertoire of recognisable strategies to become meaningful. Kofi Agawu, in his discussion of the concept of 'African rhythm', names a variety of 'culturally relevant habits' used by musicians to generate new content within existing musical structures; for instance, 'play, maneuver, tease, withhold, extend, disguise, exaggerate' (2016, 189). Such habits, adds Agawu, only become truly meaningful when they operate successfully within an existing cultural framework or 'thought regime' (190). For instance, forms of rhythmic teasing can only be appreciated if the audience has a certain understanding of the directions that a musical phrase would normally take. In other words, the expectations that shape perceptions of music, as studied in more detail by scholars such as Leonard Meyer (1956) and Maria Witek (2016), cannot exists without an understanding of musical context.

Two specific areas of musical practice in which forms of rhythmic tension and freedom commonly appear are, on the one hand, tonal movement, and, on the other, accentuation, which refers to forms of musical emphasis or stress. According to Victor Zuckerkandl, tones can suggest various forms of movement within musical time; they can overstate or understate the continuity of what he calls the 'time wave', contradict it, cross it, and also 'produce all sorts of combinations of these possibilities by doing the same or different things in the different areas' (1959, 119). Other theorists have expanded the concept of temporal movement beyond the tonal level towards other types of accentuation. Fred Lerdahl and Ray Jackendoff, for instance, distinguish between three type of accentuation in music: a phenomenal accent, which refers to any way in which a musical moment is made to stand out; a structural accent, which refers to a 'point of gravity' within the context of a phrase or section; and, thirdly, the metrical accent, which points towards the relative strength of a beat in relation to its metrical context (1983, 17). Building on the work of these scholars, Bernat Jiménez de Cisneros (2015) has provided a detailed analysis of the ways in which the performance and perception of pulses and accents at different levels contributes to the complex rhythmic experiences in flamenco.

Thus far, my discussion has outlined various musical procedures associated with rhythmic tension and freedom without considering the sociocultural dimensions of rhythm. Indeed, rhythm is often not produced by one single musical voice but rather results from the highly coordinated distribution of interlocking voices and layers of musical meaning (Denning, 2015, 194–195). Matthew Butterfield suggests, for instance, that jazz 'swing' is not only an aesthetic but also a social-interactive process, as it tends to be hard for musicians to play rhythmically without a minimal level of personal attunement (2010, 318–335). In the context of modern flamenco guitar, such divisions of rhythmic labour can be seen as both an internalised and an externalised process. In live performances and recordings, for instance, modern flamenco guitarists usually rely on a rhythm section comprised by a group of *palmeros* (clappers) alongside a modest number of percussion instruments (most commonly cajón) to lay out the basic pulse of a certain style. The presence of a rhythm section affords modern guitarists with greater freedom than previous generations of players to create tensions within the rhythmic context provided by their fellow musicians. On an individual level, however, such divisions of rhythmic labour are also reflected by the guitarist's body. For instance, guitarists can switch between different footwork patterns to evoke a specific pulse and feel (also see Jiménez de Cisneros, 2020, 210–220). Some guitarists use soundboard percussion or emphatic bodily movements and gestures to accentuate moments of rhythmic tension, especially when performing the cadence (known in flamenco as the *remate*). Recent examples are Dani de Morón's frequent uses of soundboard percussion towards the end of the cadence (see Section 4.3); Diego del Morao's typical nods with the head as a substitute for the cadence (see Section 5.3); or Yerai Cortés's movements with the right arm to build up tension before the end of the cadence.[4] In these different scenarios, then, rhythmic playfulness can emerge out of the interactions between a flamenco guitarist and other musicians, but also due to the interlocking roles of different embodied aspects of flamenco guitar playing.

Most flamenco styles, also known as *palos*, are structured around metrical forms of twelve beats. Two key styles that I will discuss in this Element are *soleares*,

---

[4] See the following performance by Yerai Cortés: www.youtube.com/watch?v=Feolgrj3aAY.

a solemn and emotive style,[5] and *bulerías*, which are more up-tempo and festive. In flamenco circles, these styles are most commonly counted as cycles consisting of twelve beats (or six beats, in the case of some varieties of bulerías) with patterns of accentuation that are relatively unfamiliar in the Western repertoire – in soleares, for instance, the emphasis commonly falls on beats twelve, three, seven, eight, and ten (also see Kliman, 2020a).[6] To translate this terminology into Western musical notation, flamenco scholars have observed that the rhythms of soleares and bulerías should both be considered as quadruple metres where the crotchet (quarter note) corresponds with one beat. In his detailed discussion of questions of musical notation, Bernat Jiménez de Cisneros defines soleares and bulerías as variable metrical structures encompassing two blocks of six beats each, where the first block is organised as a ternary metre (6/4) and the second block as a binary metre (3/2) (2015, 133–162). However, some varieties of this style, such as the *bulería al golpe* and local varieties of bulerías in cities such as Jerez, Morón or Lebrija, are more commonly counted as six-beat rather than as twelve-beat cycles (for accentuation patterns across different varieties of bulerías, see Chinoy, 2022, 335 and Rodríguez, 2014, 12). Such varieties, then, could also be described as stable ternary metres (Jiménez de Cisneros, 2015, 149–158).[7] More importantly, different ways of understanding the metrical structures of bulerías can coexist within a single performance or recording, thus leading to ambiguity, but also showing the great flexibility of this style (Jiménez de Cisneros, 2015, 153–158). Some guitarists, furthermore, draw consciously on such variations if they wish to evoke different atmospheres associated with specific places or traditions, as I discuss further in Section 4.3.

Throughout this Element, I will follow the aforementioned scholars in defining soleares and bulerías as quadruple metres, thus considering the crotchet as equivalent to one beat. As highlighted in the previous paragraph, different varieties of bulerías can be understood as shorter or longer cycles comprising six or twelve beats, depending on aspects of speed, accentuation, and feel. For the sake of consistency and clarity in the analysis, I have elected to consider both styles as twelve-beat cycles – especially since, in the work of some guitarists, the rhythmic intention behind their playing cannot always be clearly identified with a single tradition or variety of bulerías. The time signature I have employed in the

---

[5] *Soleá* is derived from the word 'solitude' (*soledad*) and traditionally evokes deep emotions such as grief and abandonment. It is one of the richest and most respected styles, both in flamenco song, where it is considered as 'the mother of cantes' (Manuel, 2006, 100), and in dance and guitar.

[6] As Bernat Jiménez de Cisneros notes, apart from metric structures and patterns of accentuation, tempo is another factor that helps distinguish between these different styles: soleares tend to oscillate between 112 and 180 bpm (if less so today than in earlier recordings), whereas the tempo of bulerías ranges from 200 to 280 bpm (2015, 42, 143, 160).

[7] I will come back to the ambiguity of the metrical structure of bulerías in Section 3.

	12	1	2	3	4	5	6	7	8	9	10	11
Soleares (two variations)	X	x	x	X	x	x	X	x	X	x	X	x
	X	x	x	X	x	x	x	X	X	x	X	x
Bulerías al 12 (two variations)	X	x	x	X	x	x	X	x	X	x	X	x
	X	x	x	X	x	x	x	X	X	x	X	x
Bulerías de Jerez		x	x	X	x	x		x	x	X	x	x
Bulerías de Morón (two variations)		x	x		x	x		x	x		x	x
	X	x	X	x	X	x	X	x	X	x	X	x

Figure 1 Metrical structures and common accentuation patterns in soleares and bulerías

musical transcriptions is 3/4, meaning that a cycle of twelve beats is comprised of four bars (where relevant, I name the bar numbers in the analysis). Thus, when referring to recurring metrical accents in the cycle (e.g. beats three or ten), the numbering refers to the position of those accents measured against the overarching structure of twelve beats. Given their importance in later parts of this study, in Figure 1 I provide a diagram with common accentuation patterns of soleares and two varieties of bulerías associated with the cities of Jerez and Morón.

Georges Didi-Huberman describes these metrical structures as the 'laws' of flamenco, a term that evokes the perspective of utmost discipline and obedience with which musicians usually adhere to them (Didi-Huberman, 2008, 90). Indeed, while it is generally acceptable for a flamenco guitarist to make minor technical mistakes or play the wrong chord, getting lost in compás is inadmissible.Therefore, the expression *tener compás* ('to have rhythm') or *tener soniquete* ('to have swing') has significant weight in flamenco culture. In Sections 2.2 and 2.3, I develop a theoretical framework that allows to think further about the suggestion that rhythm can be possessed, and more so by some than by others.

2.2 From Passive Inheritance to Active Identification

In Western discourse, rhythm has often been seen as a predominant feature of non-Western musical traditions – ranging from African and Afro-diasporic to Eastern-European contexts. In early scholarship on genres such as jazz, rhythmic skill has even been interpreted as a token of sociopolitical subversiveness. Michael Denning, in his discussion of different takes on what he calls the 'ideology of rhythm and race' (2015, 186), illustrates this process by reflecting on the concept of syncopation, which he broadly defines as 'a more or less technical term for the displacement of accents to the weak or off beat' (2015, 188). While, on a musical level, this definition overlooks stricter understandings of off-beat accentuation – for Zuckerkandl, syncopation refers to accents that fall between the beats rather than on the weak beats (1959, 118, 124) – Denning's discussion illustrates how syncopation is also meaningful as a cultural discourse. For instance, he cites the words of jazz commentator Ann Shaw Faulkner, who stated in 1921 that syncopation is 'an expression in music of the desire for that freedom which been [sic] denied to its interpreter' (2015, 189). Other critics, such as Mark Abel (2014, 149–153) and Julio Ramos (2010, 67), have made similar comments about the way that the syncope's diversion from metrical patterns has been associated with acts of defiance against an established order. Like syncopation, metre has also been subjected to political readings where it is seen as an authoritarian structure that restricts, rather than enables, the possibilities of rhythmic performance (Abel, 2014, 151). Jazz scholar Matthew Butterfield, in a way similar to Denning, outlines the racial underpinnings of this imaginary: while metre was seen by many early jazz critics as leading to the 'musical enslavement' of rhythm and thus as a token of whiteness (2010, 307), rhythm, on the other hand, was more commonly associated with variability, flexibility, and blackness.

To be sure, a number of scholars have disputed such racialised concepts of rhythm. For instance, Kofi Agawu has criticised the idea that there is a distinctive 'African' way of understanding and performing rhythm. As he notes, rhythm is not a coherent notion in all African cultures, as it is entangled, to various degrees, with other dimensions of life in different cultural and geographical contexts (1995, 388). Moreover, he observes that concepts of rhythm in African music are not fundamentally different from those existing in Western music (2016, 156). Similarly, Ronald Radano has deconstructed the notion that there are immutable essences in Black music that can be passively retained and inherited. As he notes, 'the analytical concept of "retentions" implies a historical continuity that cannot be comprehended apart from the discourses and social processes that cast this very idea into being' (2003, 10). Building on Radano's suggestion, Matthew Butterfield has argued that while identifications of musicians with an 'African' essence may be partially rooted in invented categories, this does not preclude the 'real' work they do in practices and perceptions of music (2010, 317).

From this perspective, the racial lineages and inheritances that have shaped understandings of rhythm do not necessarily correspond with a pre-existing reality and are perhaps better understood as forms of active identification. Susan Leigh Foster, in her work on two contemporary choreographers of African ancestry, explores how these performers actively recreate – or 're-member' – the 'African' element in their work by engaging critically with the legacies of colonialism. In Foster's words, these performers actively create memory of a past through their commitment to a shared vocabulary of movements. These motions resemble a past way of performing and carry with them a history of significance, but they are only made meaningful through the consensus about them that is established as dancers and viewers collectively work out what they are doing and watching (Foster, 2010, 133).

It is through these dancers' 'tactical' engagements with racial lineages, argues Foster, that they construct 'an awareness of the specificities of a place called "Africa"' (2010, 131). Mark Abel suggests in highly similar terms that the emphasis on rhythm in American popular music, which traditionally has been considered as a quintessentially 'African' inheritance, can be understood as 'an active, conscious process of identification rather than the unconscious transmission of cultural heritage by (quasi-)genetic means. As a process of selection and choice, it is obviously open to musicians of any and all backgrounds to engage in' (2014, 77).

As this discussion illustrates, rhythm is an important object of study in broader debates about the way that bodies of ancestral knowledge and cultural heritage are transmitted, retained, and actualised in the present. I have already pointed to the work of several scholars of Afro-diasporic music and performance who, in their respective discussions of rhythm, suggest that artistic and racial legacies are not so much pre-existing realities but emerge as acts of performance and identification in the present. Such insights can be fruitfully related to the work of various other scholars who, while not working specifically on rhythm, have explored the creative and generative dimensions of cultural heritage. As some heritage scholars have noted, it may seem paradoxical to suggest that musical practices that are living and mutable can somehow be safeguarded or preserved (Alivizatou, 2012, 10; Pryer, 2019, 35). Yet, as noted by Barbara Kirshenblatt-Gimblett in her influential definition of the concept, heritage 'produces something new in the present that has recourse to the past' (1995, 369–370). In a similar vein, Rodney Harrison states that heritage 'is not a "thing"' but represents 'a set of attitudes to, and relationships with the past' (2012, 14); Emma Waterton and Steve Watson theorise heritage as both a discursive system and a way of engaging with the past through cultural practices and performances (2015, 11); and the editors of the volume *Sites of Popular Music Heritage* have referred to the way that constructions and experiences of popular music *as* heritage refer to multidimensional realities with affective, material, symbolic, and performative dimensions (Cohen et al., 2015, 2).

If heritage reflects a set of relationships with the past that emerge from the perspective of the present, then this suggests that such identifications can be disputed as part of broader struggles over the meanings of the past. It is worth remembering that according to UNESCO's definition of intangible cultural heritage, included in its 2003 Convention, heritage comes into being when individuals and groups acknowledge it as such: '[t]he "intangible cultural heritage" means the practices, representations, expressions, knowledge, skills – as well as the instruments, objects, artefacts and cultural spaces associated therewith – that communities, groups and, in some cases, individuals recognise as part of their cultural heritage' (qtd. Pryer, 2019, 28). What remains unacknowledged in this definition, however, is that there may be complex reasons for which open-ended and living cultural forms may become recognisable (or not) as heritage and may subsequently be inscribed (or not) into official and unofficial discourses about the past, tradition, and authenticity. The second half of UNESCO's definition, moreover, suggests that heritage is open to newness and recreation: 'This intangible cultural heritage, transmitted from generation to generation, is constantly recreated by communities and groups in response to their environment, their interaction with nature and their history, and provides them with a sense of identity and continuity, thus promoting respect for cultural diversity and human creativity' (qtd. Pryer, 2019, 28). The fact that heritage is constantly actualised further shows that the recognisability of a cultural phenomenon as heritage can change over time.

Francisco Aix Gracia's work on different positionalities towards heritage in flamenco (2014) offers a helpful framework to think more critically about the complex reasons that may shape the identifications with heritage of different individuals and groups. Building on Michel de Certeau's (1984) distinction between 'strategies' and 'tactics', Aix Gracia explores the role of concepts of heritage across a variety of official and unofficial contexts in flamenco culture. Strategic uses of heritage, he explains, are those that emerge from a clearly identifiable locus of power – for instance, the heritage agendas of Andalusia's regional government. Tactical uses of heritage, on the other hand, refer to the more or less organised manner in which individual artists may position themselves towards specific elements from the flamenco repertoire and inscribe those elements into a certain understanding of the 'tradition' (2014, 126–127). One example of this process is the way that flamenco musicians tend to position themselves as followers of influential artists from the past – for example, those who follow the influential Gitano singer Antonio Mairena are called *mairenistas*, while those whose voices resemble that of the even more popular flamenco singer Camarón de la Isla are known as *camaroneros*. By adopting specific elements of the repertoire as more meaningful than others, continues Aix Gracia, artists also establish their own positionality as one of 'inheritors' or 'debtors' of the tradition. For Aix Gracia, such identifications do not emerge in a vacuum but depend on the availability of different types of material, social, and symbolical capital (128). For instance, someone who has grown up in a city or family that has strong connections with flamenco can establish such identifications more easily than someone who enters flamenco culture with no initial relation to it. For Aix Gracia, then, identifications with music as heritage are not open and available to all – or at least not to the same degree.[8]

This distinction between strategic and tactical identifications sheds light on the various reasons that may move individuals to 'recognise' elements of a musical repertoire as part of their heritage. At first glance, in the increasingly transnational contexts in which flamenco circulates today, understandings of rhythmic skill as a type of local heritage may merely seem obsolete or nostalgic references to a time when this music was more clearly at home at the local level. However, in certain contexts, such concepts can be better understood as tactical responses to institutional and commercial pressures, as well as to historical forms of repression and marginalisation of Gitanos and other flamenco practitioners.[9] For example, Matthew Machin-Autenrieth has noted that an emphasis on the local idiosyncrasies of flamenco can afford artists with the 'discursive basis' to validate their musical practices, especially when attempting to capture institutional support and funding in a competitive heritage industry (2017, 165). In the specific case of the Spanish Roma people, scholars have aimed to devolve critical agency to Gitanos in acknowledgement not only of their repression and marginalisation by different regimes in Spanish history but also since their cultural practices have repeatedly been appropriated (Charnon-Deutsch, 2004; Periáñez, 2023; Woods Peiró, 2012). Such appropriations of Romani culture in Spain and beyond have led to racialised essentialisations of rhythmic skill – as reflected in the concept of 'gypsy rhythm' (Denning, 2015, 187) – that are radically different from the localised understandings of rhythm held by the Roma people themselves (Periáñez, 2023, 147–164). These examples indicate that identifications with heritage are far from consensus-based but rather operate in a complex forcefield shaped by a variety of cultural, economic, and political interests.

2.3 From Identification to Open-Endedness

Beyond the discursive disputes over heritage discussed in the previous section, some of the aforementioned scholars have also suggested that relations with

---

[8] This does not mean, however, that the availability of different forms of capital leads automatically to the establishment of such identifications. In later parts of this Element, I will pay careful attention to the ways in which flamenco guitarists who come from sociocultural environments with strong connections to rhythm may nonetheless cast doubts on oversimplified references to rhythm as part of their local heritage.

[9] To name an example from outside flamenco culture, the work of the Senegalese intellectual and politician Léopold Sédar Senghor is named by several scholars as an example of how identifications with an essentialised notion of 'African rhythm' has also contributed to decolonial projects (Barletta, 2020, 111–115; Diouf & Kiddoe Nwankwo, 2010a, 10–11).

heritage are established on the level of artistic performance. What, then, can rhythm contribute to discussions about the ways in which such artistic identifications with cultural heritage take shape? To answer this question, I would like to expand on my earlier discussion of rhythm and its reliance on both preexisting structures and irregularity. Based on this dynamic, I suggest that rhythm can establish musical identifications with past repertoires but also gesture towards open-ended forms of communion and communication.

In her monograph *Fado Resounding*, Lila Ellen Gray introduces the concept of 'cumulative listening' to better understand how fado performers and instrumentalists constantly actualise and recreate conventional elements from a preexisting repertoire of melodic pathways. The attuned listener, Gray suggests, will be able to appreciate such actualisations of previous renderings of fado and can use them to establish affective relations between present performances and bygone places and times. Gray theorises this act of 'cumulative listening' as

> a listening that includes past renderings of the same traditional fado structure in the inner ear, a listening that juxtaposes the styling one hears in the present with the styling one remembers by a different performer in the past, a performance located in a specific time-place. Traditional fado structure facilitates an overdetermined relation to past listenings, a suturing of the multiple stories told by lyrics to particular musical forms, to specific traditional fado 'musical bases'. (Gray, 2013, 156–157)

Building on Gray's concept, Joshua Brown has noted that similar forms of sedimentation exist in flamenco. Flamenco artists, like fado musicians, operate within 'established rhythmic, melodic, harmonic and poetic frameworks' that are constantly 'reinscribed with new melodies and approaches that are received aurally, and often visually, in the context of previously experienced performances' (2014, 78). In flamenco guitar, continues Brown, recurrent styles and *falsetas* (melodic passages or micro-compositions) can be thought of as portals to the past; they operate as 'mechanisms of historical continuity' as they 'bring attention, and inscribe new meanings, to the sounds connected with specific localities and artists' (78). Thus, artists and listeners constantly negotiate their position towards existing repertoires of musical knowledge; or as Brown notes, flamenco musicians 're-present and re-produce tradition through sonically articulated affiliations' (78).

The cultural habits that musicians rely on to establish rhythmic tension within a temporal framework can be thought of as yet another mechanism of historical continuity, similar to those discussed by Brown. Admittedly, operating creatively within a given temporal structure is not necessarily the same as establishing a relation with past renderings of that same structure. However, Gray and Brown draw attention to the fact that any performance of fado or flamenco is always, to an extent, palimpsestic, as both musicians and listeners aurally inscribe present performances into recognisable musical forms, thus establishing specific musical and affective relations between the present and the past.[10]

Such inscriptions may be complicated, however, by rhythm's tendency towards tension and irregularity. To develop this argument, I wish to briefly dwell on a work of flamenco scholarship by the art philosopher Georges Didi-Huberman. In it, I find elements of an innovative critical vocabulary that makes rhythm thinkable as an open-ended communicative force. In his study *El bailaor de soledades* (2008), which meditates on the avant-garde flamenco dancer Israel Galván, Didi-Huberman brings together a varied collection of critical traditions, such as philosophies of time and rhythm and critical work on bullfighting, to theorise several elusive concepts that circulate widely in discourses about bullfighting as well as flamenco. I focus here on Didi-Huberman's discussion of two key terms: *gracia* ('grace') and *temple* – a polysemic and untranslatable term that is semantically entangled with verbs such as 'to place in agreement with each other', 'to harmonize', or 'to temper' (2008, 144). In Didi-Huberman's work, both concepts refer to the ways that the dancing body interacts organically with its spatial environments and with the temporal coordinates of music. If a dancer performs with grace, suggests Didi-Huberman, it almost appears as if the rhythm 'obeys' the dancing body (95). However, in later parts of his study, Didi-Huberman problematises the dancer's relationship with rhythm as one of outright control. When delving into the concept of temple, he notes that being in control of rhythm is not necessarily an act of complete possession, but rather one of respectful communication and mutual attunement (166–170). Furthermore, by evoking such concepts of interlocution and communication, this scholar suggest that rhythm cannot be fully possessed by the dancer and partially remains an external force. This suggestion is reminiscent of the work of Pierre Sauvanet, who also notes that rhythm cannot be clearly located outside or inside the musician; one's possession *of* rhythm is always simultaneously a possession *by* it (2000, 132–138). For Sauvanet, similar to Didi-Huberman, rhythm is a 'magnetic field' or 'forcefield' (136) that partially takes over the body whilst maintaining a position of semi-autonomy.

In this context, the concept of temple attains further meaning as a form of communion. In his reading of Israel Galván's performance *Arena*,[11] which draws on the kinaesthetic vocabulary of bullfighting, Didi-Huberman explores how the dancer's gestures and movements invoke the figure of an imaginary bull that is not physically present on stage (2008, 160–164). Beyond the cultural

---

[10] The concepts of dialogue and communication employed by Gray and Brown have also been used in scholarship on jazz improvisation (see Berliner, 1994).

[11] 'Arena' refers to bull ring as well as to sand.

context of bullfighting, Didi-Huberman suggests that Galván's performances of flamenco dance tend to invoke an absent addressee – invocations that can be thought of in both aesthetic and ethical terms. Indeed, the title of Didi-Huberman's study refers to the figure of a 'dancer of solitudes' – someone who, even when not accompanied by other musicians, is not alone. This dancer converts their own solitude into a figure, a gestalt, and is thus able to be alone and in communion at the same time. Thus, Didi-Huberman's work casts an original light on the intersections between rhythm and embodiment by framing this relationship not through the common semantics of power (mastery, domin-ion, control, enslavement), but rather as an intimate relationship between a Self and Other. Crucially, this semantics of rhythm also resists common inscriptions of movements and gestures into sedimented frameworks of mean-ing. As Didi-Huberman suggests, not every rhythmic gesture can be easily validated by ('legislar') or made to obey to pre-existing structures (161). From his perspective, rhythm is an act of communion and communication where none of the single entities (bullfighter or bull; the solo dancer or their absent addressee) dominates the other. Rather, when approached from within an ethical framework, it is rhythm itself that holds sway over both: 'rhythm – this way of being together in time – will then reign as lord and master over the two associated solitudes' ('el ritmo – esa manera de estar juntos en el tiempo – reina entonces como dueño y señor de ambas soledades compañeras') (162).[12]

As Didi-Huberman suggests here, perhaps rhythm does not have to be possessed by anyone to be culturally meaningful. If we consider rhythm as maintaining a semi-autonomous position towards the musician(s) who enter in its forcefield – or put in ethical terms, as having the position of an Other – then it can also facilitate more open-ended forms of communication. To an extent, Didi-Huberman's reading of rhythm in terms of resistance is reminiscent of the historical associations between rhythm and disobedience that I have explored on earlier pages. By recalling that historical discourse here, I am not aiming for a renewed cultural essentialisation of rhythm. Rather, rhythm emerges from Didi-Huberman's work as resistant to any type of discursive inscription or, in his terminology, 'validation'. From this perspective, rhythm can be thought of as operating at the intersection between identification and radical openness.

It is this intersection, I propose, that also affords new ways of thinking about the relation between rhythm and heritage. If rhythmic practices are considered not only as sedimented but also as open-ended, then they have the potential to bring about what some scholars have called 'emergent' and 'future-oriented'

---

[12] For an exploration of the possible ethical aspects of this rapport between the *matador* and bull that resonates with Didi-Huberman's discussion, see De Haro De San Mateo and Marvin (2015).

types of heritage. William Washabaugh, for instance, proposes a reading of flamenco as 'a thing yet to be achieved, an aspiration' (2012, 10). Similarly, Valeria Loiacono and Julia Fallon, in their work on the transnational dynamics of belly dance (*Raqs sharqi*), emphasise how heritage should be thought of as an ever-shifting framework of cultural meaning that is constantly inscribed and reinscribed with new meanings through the lived experiences and cultural mobility of the individuals who practise it (2018, 288–289). Rhythm, I argue, is another way in which the sedimented cultural meanings of music can get affirmed but also extended and challenged. As Didi-Huberman acknowledges, rhythm can push towards the limits of recognisability, and perhaps we should therefore refrain from 'suturing' all its complex manifestations, to recall Gray's terminology, to pre-existing frameworks of musical meaning. In the next sections, I further examine how discourses and practices of rhythm in modern flamenco guitar gesture towards concepts of cultural heritage that may be defined as emergent and open-ended.

3 Jerez de la Frontera

3.1 Rhythmic Places

Most flamenco styles are strongly associated with specific histories and localities in Andalusia. References to iconic locations and neighbourhoods, such as Sacromonte in Granada, Triana in Seville, or Santiago and San Miguel in Jerez, figure prominently in the lyrics of flamenco song and in associated discourses about origins and authenticity. Other villages, cities, and regions may lack an explicit, verbal presence in flamenco, but can nonetheless be conjured up through other elements in musical performance. As Clara Chinoy notes, subtle variations in tempo and accentuation in performances of bulerías are important markers of geographical and identitarian difference (2022, 336). Matthew Machin-Autenrieth has explored, moreover, how concepts of locality are articulated through artistic discourses and musical practices in the city of Granada, including through performances and pedagogies of flamenco guitar (2017, 143–166).

The following two sections explore the relations between rhythm and place-based concepts of heritage in the Andalusian cities of Jerez and Morón. I examine how these cities have emerged as hubs of flamenco guitar performance and, in particular, as places associated with distinctively rhythmic types of playing. I will argue that localised concepts of rhythmic feel are complex imaginaries that are part based on tangible varieties in uses of guitar technique and sedimented accentuation patterns, but also partially on more elusive identities, lineages, and affiliations. In this respect, I follow Machin-Autenrieth's assertion that the concept of a local 'school' of guitar playing in Granada 'is representative of an idealised narrative of local history, heritage and artistic lineages' (2017, 165). Similarly, in the context of Jerez and Morón, I examine how different modern flamenco musicians negotiate assertions about the local feel of rhythm in a variety of artistic and pedagogical settings.[13]

3.2 Rhythm in Jerez: *Soniquete* as Cultural Discourse

As I noted in the Introduction, soniquete broadly refers to rhythmic feel or swing in flamenco. While it is widely used in flamenco parlance, on the following pages I explore how the term attains specific local meanings in discourses about rhythm in Jerez. I start here with a brief etymological discussion of the relations between soniquete and rhythm. According to the *Diccionario crítico etimológico de la lengua castellana*, soniquete is a derivative of *son* and *sonar*, which both originate in the Latin root *sonare* and broadly refer to sound. The *Diccionario de la Real Academia Española* and María Moliner's *Diccionario del uso del español*, on the other hand, both define soniquete as a pejorative form of *son* and compare it to the word *sonsonete*, which refers to an unpleasant sound that is monotonously repeated. In the specific context of flamenco, however, *son* is also commonly used as a synonym for rhythm. According to José Manuel Gamboa and Faustino Núñez, soniquete is the diminutive – rather than pejorative – form of *son*, a term that refers, in this context, to the percussive movements of the hands and feet used to perform specific accents (2007, 530). For these scholars, soniquete 'refers to the airiness, to the internalised flamenco rhythm shown by an artist or in a certain performance, especially in the festive styles' (531).[14]

The term soniquete appears with particular frequency in discourses about rhythm in Jerez. For instance, Bernat Jiménez de Cisneros has transcribed a series of testimonies from different palmeros who associate ways of clapping in Jerez more commonly with soniquete than clapping patterns and techniques in Seville, despite their claim that such patterns tend to be more virtuosic in the latter city than in the former (Jiménez de Cisneros, 2020, 323–325). Furthermore, the

---

[13] By focusing on these locations, I do not wish to subdue the importance of other flamenco guitar traditions, such as that in Granada (González, 2021; Machin-Autenrieth, 2017, 143–166). Rather, my selection is based on the fact that, in opposition to other guitar traditions or schools, Jerez and Morón are more commonly associated with rhythm. In future work, this analysis could be expanded towards other areas, such as the Caño Roto neighbourhood in Madrid, which is home to a rich and virtuosic flamenco guitar tradition that is also commonly associated with a distinctive type of 'swing'.

[14] Antonio Mairena and Ricardo Molina (1963) claimed that, prior to the incorporation of the guitar into flamenco, rhythmic deep song styles would be accompanied exclusively by '"the son" or palmas, percussive accents made with the knuckles, feet or heels' (qtd. Rioja, 1995a, 12). Budasz (2007, 6–8) explains that, in the early-modern Ibero-Atlantic world, the Portuguese word *som* was commonly used as a term for instrumental guitar pieces.

flamenco guitarist Moraíto (1947–2011), who remains one of the most celebrated flamenco musicians from Jerez despite his early death, has stated that what distinguishes guitar playing in his city from other local traditions is 'el soniquete', by which he means 'the way of carrying the rhythm' ('la manera de llevar el compás') (Álvarez Caballero, 2003, 298). Similarly, flamenco scholar Norberto Torres Cortés, in his analysis of Moraíto's playing, states that soniquete refers to the 'rhythmic games played by youngsters in Jerez's artistic neighbourhoods, especially when performing a bulería' (2012, 59n4).

Within Jerez, it is possible to delineate an even more specific location associated with rhythm: the neighbourhood of Santiago, which is situated in the north of the city and has historically known a high density of flamenco artists. According to flamenco scholar José María Castaño, artists from Santiago have had an unmatched ability to combine flamenco with refreshing and ever-evolving rhythmic and musical elements – a skill that, he argues, cannot be found to the same degree in Jerez's other flamenco neighbourhood, known alternatively as San Miguel or La Plazuela (2005, 409). Similarly, in an episode entitled 'The Neighbourhood of Santiago', aired in February 1972 on Spanish state television as part of the documentary series *Rito y geografía del cante* (*Rite and Geography of Flamenco Song*), the flamenco singer Tío Borrico and other local artists discuss the vivid artistic atmosphere that has existed in Santiago. When remembering the time of his parents, Tío Borrico claims that Santiago had an atmosphere and rhythm ('son') that has not existed anywhere else in Spain ('los entornos de ese Santiago y el son de ese Santiago no lo ha habido en España entera') (22:28).[15] More recently, in a brief rhythm workshop delivered on YouTube, the palmero and percussionist Manuel Cantarote, who was born in Santiago, draws in a creative way on an expression that was popularised by the multidisciplinary flamenco artist Diego Carrasco, stating that the rhythm of bulerías should be understood as a 'biorhythm' ('biorritmo').[16] Carrasco, who is from the same neighbourhood, originally used this term in a newspaper interview, stating that 'compás is like the course of a river, you have it or you don't; a matter of biorhythm' (Seisdedos, 2017). Building freely on this concept, Cantarote notes that this is a type of rhythm that emanates directly from the body. As he claims, palmas need to be aligned with and supported by footwork, sideway movements of the torso, and breathing techniques to be performed properly. While Cantarote uses biorhythm as a concept for internalised and embodied rhythmic performance, he also suggests that this type of clapping allows one to tap into Santiago's distinctive rhythmic atmosphere: 'and that is

---

[15] The episode can be retrieved here: www.rtve.es/play/videos/rito-y-geografia-del-cante/rito-geo grafia-del-cante-barrio-santiago/4682278/.

[16] Manuel Cantarote's video can be retrieved here: www.youtube.com/watch?v=ATK_6IWMPlc.

where our biorhythm from Santiago starts to appear' ('y ahí ya empieza ya [sic] el biorritmo de nosotros de aquí de Santiago'). In other words, rhythmic clapping emerges from Cantarote's words as a performance of local heritage.

3.3 Rhythm in the Morao Family

One of the most prominent flamenco families from Santiago are known as Los Morao. The first influential figure from this family, who is also often named as the most important contributor to a local school of guitar playing in Jerez, is Manuel Moreno Jiménez (born 1929), better known as Manuel Morao. Morao studied extensively with Javier Molina (1868–1956), who belongs to the second generation of guitarists in Spain that cultivated the flamenco guitar as an instrument with its own distinctive style, technique, and repertoire. Molina, in his turn, was mentored by two late nineteenth-century guitarists: Paco el Barbero, a disciple of José González Patiño (also known as Maestro Patiño) (Rioja, 1995e, 168–169; Torres, 2012, 66–68; Vega, 1995, 143–145); and Rafael Barroso, a pioneering flamenco guitarist from Jerez (Rioja, 1995d, 162; Torres, 2012, 67). Unlike some of the more virtuosic flamenco guitarists from the late nineteenth century, Molina and his teachers did not draw extensively on the sophisticated repertoires and techniques from the classical guitar. Rather, their playing revolved around thumb and strumming techniques and around rhythmic flamenco styles such as bulerías, *soleá por bulerías* and *siguiriyas* (Vital, 2020). One influential element of Molina's style is an archaic variety of the *alzapúa* technique, which is directed at the creation of rhythmic counterpoint effects with the thumb and index finger. Today, most flamenco guitarists perform this mechanism exclusively with upward and downward strokes of the thumb; however, the older dynamic between the thumb and index is still widely used in Jerez, thus lending a distinctive signature to the city's guitar tradition.[17]

The emergence of a rhythmic type of guitar playing in Jerez is, however, mostly posterior to Molina and more commonly attributed to Manuel Morao.[18] Apart from numerous flamenco scholars, guitarists, and teachers, Manuel Morao himself has also insistently drawn attention to his pioneering role in

---

[17] For a study of old and modern varieties of alzapúa, with transcriptions and audio examples, see Kliman, 2023. In a brief tutorial on YouTube (www.youtube.com/watch?v=Umfu3fZd8Qs), Diego del Morao, the most prominent member of the present generation of guitarists from the Morao family, explains how various alternations between the thumb and index finger can be combined when performing this technique. Another player from Jerez who uses intricate patterns of alzapúa is Manuel Parrilla, as illustrated at 2:15 in the following video: www.youtube.com/watch?v=fOkJyGtdA50.

[18] The Jerez-born guitarist El Carbonero (qtd. Torres, 2012, 71) considers Manuel Morao a stronger contributor than Molina to the formation of a guitar school in Jerez. From his perspective, Molina's work can be associated with the formation of a proto-school.

establishing a distinctively rhythmic way of playing in Jerez. In his biography, penned by Juan Manuel Suárez Japón, Morao explains that he created a specific way of accompanying bulería that had greater depth and complexity ('gran dificultad') than earlier forms as it involved more elaborate patterns of accentuation (2014, 230–233). In a later interview included in the same publication, Morao laments the early death of his nephew Moraíto, whom he considered the true heir of this rhythmic style ('Era dueño de un ritmo que era el nuestro') (430). Importantly, Morao's allusion to a shared rhythmic heritage operates at the intersection of family, social, and ethnic bonds. On one level, he describes this heritage as belonging to 'the Morao dynasty' ('la saga de los Morao'), thus suggesting that rhythmic skill is transmitted along what Francisco Bethencourt Llobet names 'patrilineal' routes of influence (2011, 108). However, Morao also relates this rhythmic heritage to the Jerez guitar school ('la escuela jerezana') and, more broadly, to the Spanish Roma people who have contributed to the consolidation of what he calls 'flamenco gitano andaluz' (431). Thus, Morao's discourse about the local dynamics of rhythm builds on overlapping and intersecting concepts of lineage and heritage.

A concept that emerges from Morao's discussion as key to his contributions to rhythmic guitar playing in Jerez is *contratiempo*, which can be broadly translated as weak-beat accentuation. In an interview with Ángel Álvarez Caballero, Manuel Morao claims that he was the first to employ contratiempo in a systematic manner. He subsequently criticises contemporary practices of bulería as lacking in depth, either for having abandoned the accentuation patterns he helped establish or, alternatively, for recurring too frequently to weak-beat accentuation. In another interview with Juan Manuel Suárez Japón, he identifies such contemporary ways of practising bulería not with contratiempo but with soniquete. Here, it is worth citing the artist at length:

> I believe that what most characterizes me are the rhythmic styles, the rhythm that I understood in a different way, I started playing lots of contratiempos that now are widely practiced, I even think they are now played too much, but I was the first to propose new ways of playing these styles that were very simple, and started complicating them a bit further through contratiempo. (Álvarez Caballero, 2003, 74).
>
> A few weeks ago I was at a wedding [...] A number of Gitanos from the present generation were there and at one point some started singing and then I listened carefully and said to a friend: this is what the rhythm of the *bulería de Jerez* has become, coarse and monotonous, a soniquete, they now call it that way, soniquete, like saying something nice about it, without knowing that this isn't true! This is what we've ended up with, my friend! (Suárez Japón, 2014, 232)

A detailed look at Morao's uses of rhythmic concepts such as contratiempo and soniquete reveals that these are part not only of a musical but also of a decidedly emotional discourse. From an analytical perspective, when Morao critiques later generations of players for overusing contratiempo, it would appear that he refers to a rhythmic tendency that is more similar to syncopation – a rhythmic principle where, following Zuckerkandl's definition of the term (1959, 118), accents are placed between the beats – than to weak-beat accentuation. Beyond the ambiguity of his terminology on a musical level, Morao's discourse also evinces a sense of nostalgia for the past – associated here with the profundity of contratiempo and uncomprehended by present generations who are more inclined, in Morao's view, towards the levity of soniquete. On another emotional level, the term contratiempo also seems to be determined by the guitarist's pride for his own contributions to guitar playing and the hope that said contributions will be safeguarded.

More broadly, Manuel Morao's reflections about rhythmic guitar playing in Jerez engage actively with questions of recognisability and identification – questions that, as I explored in Section 2, are key to understandings of rhythm as heritage. When do performances of bulerías adhere faithfully to principles of contratiempo, and when are they excessively inclined towards the more recent concept of soniquete that, at least for Morao, appears to make the idiosyncrasies of this local style partially unrecognisable? And to what extent might the tensions between such conflicting rhythmic concepts present themselves on the level of musical practice, even within his own family? With these questions in mind, I will now explore some of the rhythmic principles that underpin Morao's own playing, as well as that of later guitarists in his family. As a case study, I start here with Manuel Morao's performance of a bulería alongside the singer Terremoto de Jerez in an episode from the aforementioned documentary series *Rito y geografía del cante*, broadcast on 9 October 1972.[19]

Normal Paul Kliman (2020b) has transcribed several variations in Manuel Morao's way of maintaining a basic bulería rhythm through a combination of strokes with the right-hand index finger, taps on the guitar soundboard, and strumming. As Kliman observes, Morao tends to flick the index from behind the thumb, a technique that, combined with a dampening of the strings by the left hand, adds a distinctive staccato effect at the end of each twelve-beat cycle. In addition to Kliman's analysis, another recurring component in Morao's playing is the systematic accentuation of beats ten and eleven of the bulería, a procedure that replaces an arguably more common accentuation pattern where beat ten (traditionally a metrical accent) receives emphasis, while beat eleven remains

---

[19] www.youtube.com/watch?v=nMZiHKTHns8

Figure 2 Manuel Morao's accentuation of beats ten and eleven in the bulería

silent. In his playing alongside Terremoto, and as illustrated in Figure 2, Morao frequently combines a rhythmic accent on beat ten, performed as a *rasgueo* (percussive strumming with different fingers of the right hand), with a downward stroke of the index finger on beat eleven.[20]

By displacing or duplicating the endings on beats ten and eleven, Morao leaves shorter silences between the common metrical accents on beats ten and twelve. As flamenco scholar Bernat Jiménez de Cisneros notes, placing rhythmic emphasis on weak beats tends to suggest a sense of movement and impulse (2015, 47), similar to what jazz scholars have named a 'forward-propelling directionality' (see Butterfield, 2010, 301–307). In Morao's playing, elements of this propulsive force are present not only on the level of metrical accentuation but also in his way of performing the chord changes in his accompaniment of the singer. Usually, when accompanying bulerías, flamenco guitarists mark the melodic change that occurs in the second of the three verses – a moment known as *cambio* – by playing the semicadence C7-F before resolving to Bb-A (dominant and tonic) in the third verse.[21] In Manuel Morao's rendering of this progression, however, he inverts the chord change by playing F and C7 instead of C7 and F. This harmonic choice undermines the resolutive strength of the semicadence: the metrical accent on beat ten now coincides with the dominant chord (C7) of the temporary tonic (F) rather than with the temporary tonic itself (also see Granados, 2004, 61). Thus, while on one level the guitarist weakens the metrical accent on beat ten, he also creates harmonic tension that induces the singer's subsequent resolution of the verse with even greater energy.

As can be seen in Figure 3, Morao uses two identical strumming patterns to mark the change from F to C7 and then the resolution from Bb to A. However, on various occasions in the performance (see 1:44 and 4:19), Morao does not

---

[20] As indicated in the Introduction, the asterisks in the transcriptions refer to soundboard taps or *golpes*.

[21] Here and on later pages, I use the chord names in relation to the tonic in which these flamenco styles are commonly performed (in the case of bulerías, A Phrygian), even though most guitarists perform the style with a capo, depending on the pitch and preference of the vocalist. In other words, different chord names are needed when considering these performances at concert pitch. Where relevant, I have indicated the position of the capo in the transcriptions.

Figure 3 Morao's performance of a semicadence and cadence (1:42–1:45)

Figure 4 Morao and Terremoto perform the cadence at the same time (5:07–5:10)

return to the tonic on beat ten but maintains a Bb chord. Once more, this is a subtle harmonic choice that deemphasises the resolutive force of the cadence and helps build on this energy in subsequent parts of the performance. A final procedure with a similar effect, both here and elsewhere in the video, is Morao's performance of the cadence before the singer, shown when he resolves to A Phrygian and introduces a new *paseo* (a strumming passage repeated between verses to maintain the rhythm) before the singer has finished the melody. Only on one occasion right at the end of the performance, as illustrated in Figure 4, does Morao finish with the singer rather than anticipating the cadence.

There is a difficulty of transcription in these different examples since, as mentioned in Section 2.1, some varieties of bulerías do not follow a stable twelve-beat pattern and can also be thought of as a six-beat cycle. Jiménez de Cisneros describes this feature as a tension between the metric and hypermetric levels

(2015, 6–8) that, in the specific case of bulerías, illustrates the syntactical ambiguity of this style (2015, 150–159, 298–299). In line with Jiménez de Cisneros's analysis, the examples from Manuel Morao's playing illustrate that different understandings of the hypermetric level can motivate different musical choices, such as the decision to anticipate the cadence. I suspect that Morao has these different types of accentual displacement in mind when discussing his contributions to rhythmic playing in Jerez, as encapsulated by his concept of contratiempo.

Later generations of guitarists in Manuel Morao's family have further developed the expressive possibilities of accentual displacement and, perhaps more so than Manuel Morao himself, syncopation. One popular example of syncopation can be found in a strumming passage that was often performed in preparation for the cadence by Manuel Morao's nephew, Moraíto, and further elaborated by the latter's son, Diego del Morao. This passage can be heard on Moraíto's composition 'Buleriando' (*Morao y oro*, 1992) as well as in numerous live performances. As shown in Figure 5, it starts with a repeated chord progression between Bb and C before resolving to the tonic. Diego del Morao occasionally performs a syncopated version of this sequence which commences one beat later than the original version and then 'remedies' that displaced start in the repetition of the chord cycle – see, for instance, Diego del Morao's playing for the flamenco singer Arcángel on 'Fuenteherida' (included on the latter's album *Tablao*, 2015).

Another iconic cadence by Moraíto that has been subject to extensive creative elaborations by Diego del Morao consists of a sequence of syncopated strokes of the index finger over an A chord, followed by a series of explosive uses of rasgueo in combination with a dampening of the strings by the left hand.[22] On a structural level, this cadence (bars 5–8 in Figure 6) can be seen as an extension of an earlier cadence (bar 4). Diego del Morao briefly alludes to this curiosity in an online guitar workshop published on the website Buscadores Flamencos, owned by flamenco guitarist and pedagogue Pituquete. In a collection of lessons about the flamenco guitar in Jerez that can be purchased on this website, Diego del Morao struggles to find an adequate term for this extended cadence – he suggests 'latiguillo' ('slap' or 'punch') or 'sobrecierre' ('extra ending') – but notes that, while this principle is now widely used by most flamenco guitarists, it was first introduced by his father.[23]

---

[22] Diego del Morao commonly performs the same remate (see Antonio Reyes, 'Bulerías', 15:07–15:12, on *Directo en el Círculo Flamenco de Madrid*, 2015) but has also developed subtle variations of it with different types of syncopation (see Antonio Reyes, 'Bulerías', 17:14–17:18, on *Directo en el Círculo Flamenco de Madrid*).

[23] These videos are available on https://buscadoresflamencos.com/producto/diego-del-morao/. Diego del Morao makes this comment in section 5.1 of the workshop.

Figure 5 Comparison of a falseta by Moraíto (1:30–1:37 on 'Buleriando') and its elaboration by Diego del Morao (5:34–5:44 on 'Fuenteherida' by singer Árcangel)

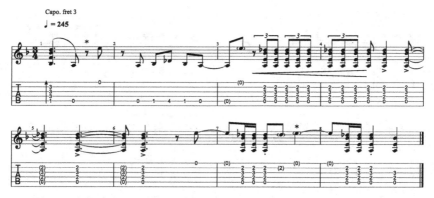

Figure 6 Cadence performed by Moraíto in 'Sor bulería' (0:53–0:57)

Thus far, my comparison of the work of three generations of players from the Morao family has focused on different types of accentual displacement. Another relevant aspect of their playing refers to the relation between rhythm and technique. This relation is highlighted by Alain Faucher, who has noted that modern flamenco guitarists such as Moraíto achieve a sense of swing by 'dampening the strings', which creates the 'sensation of a bounce' (1996, 11). A similar kinaesthetic metaphor is applied by Norberto Torres Cortés who, with reference to Moraíto's playing, characterises soniquete as a 'festive balancing act, full of humour, which people in Jerez preserve as the essence of their city' (2012, 72). To be sure, references to bodily movement frequently appear in critical discourses about rhythm. Vincent Barletta, for instance, cites the words of John Coltrane, who compared falling off rhythm with falling down an elevator shaft (2020, xii). Similarly, Georges Didi-Huberman, in his discussion of micro-timing in the work of Israel Galván, indicating how this dancer often moves towards points where the rhythm appears to get completely lost and suspended, only then to be picked up again (2008, 90, 97). In these different scenarios, the playful and even humorous effects of rhythm emerge precisely due to a skilful projection of potential imbalances by the performer's body. In the case of guitar playing, such metaphors invite for further reflections on the way in which playful movements are simulated through specific types of fingering, timbre, and attack, similar to J. Bradford Robinson's claim that the forward propulsion of jazz swing tends to be a product of a variety of interlocking manipulations of timing, volume, and physicality, such as 'timbre, attack, vibrato, intonation, or other means' (qtd. Butterfield, 2010, 301).

Among the three generations of players in the Morao family that I have examined here, Diego del Morao is perhaps the clearest example of how what

Figure 7 Moraíto's performance of a cadence in 'Buleriando' (0:36–0:38)

Dylon Robbins calls the 'corporeal, physiological realities of the popular performer' (2015, 89) make themselves visible and audible in flamenco guitar playing. This can be illustrated through a comparison of two variations of a cadence commonly performed by Moraíto and further elaborated by Diego del Morao. In Moraíto's original rendering of this sequence in his track 'Buleriando', he uses a relatively limited number of techniques of the left and right hand. After a soundboard tap, he performs a downward chromatic movement from C to Cb with short attacks of the index finger (bar 1 in Figure 7). Subsequently, he finishes the cadence by strumming over a Bb and A chord between beats seven and ten (bars 3 and 4).

Diego del Morao's version of this cadence in 'Bulería pa Jeré' (0:22–0:24), a recording made with the singer Agujetas Chico on the latter's album *Los Cuchillos del Tiempo* (2015), exhibits a much broader exploration of technique and timbre than that of Moraíto, such as uses of hammer-ons and slides at the start of the chromatic chord cycle (bar 4 in Figure 8) and a syncopated downward stroke of the thumb followed by a soundboard tap to mark the cadence (bar 7). Like other contemporary guitarists, Diego del Morao frequently mutes the resolution to the tonic by substituting it for a soundboard tap – a procedure that, while perhaps not directly inspired by his forebearers, reflects an effort to deemphasise the resolutive force of the cadence in a way similar to Manuel Morao's playing.

One of the richest illustrations of how Diego del Morao's playing is infused with manipulations of timbre and attack can be found in a falseta in the style of bulería and composed in the key of E Phrygian. While, at the time of writing, this composition has not yet been recorded as a solo piece, different versions of it can be heard on a homage to Moraíto by the Jerez-born artist Diego Carrasco ('Morao del alma' on *Hippytano*, 2012) and on a recent recording by flamenco singer Israel Fernández, with whom Diego del Morao regularly performs and records as an accompaniment guitarist ('Al Tercer Mundo', on *Pura Sangre*, 2023).[24] In the

---

[24] Different live performances of the same composition can be seen at www.youtube.com/watch?v=UCA3vOkWTd0 (from 7:24) and www.youtube.com/watch?v=B-mnsDxXmHs (from 0:50).

Figure 8 Diego del Morao's performance of a cadence in 'Bulería pa Jeré',
Agujetas Chico, *Los Cuchillos del Tiempo*, (0:22–0:24)

first part of this composition, Diego del Morao builds on a melody that is often
attributed to his great-uncle Manuel Morao.[25] Diego del Morao combines this
traditional phrase, performed with a thumb technique on the bass strings, with
a series of modern-sounding chord voicings in the build-up to a cadence. Towards
the end, the melody loses prominence as the guitarist introduces a series of
manipulations of timbre that lead to astonishing rhythmic effects. These include
staccato attacks of the strings with the right-hand index finger and playful uses of
buzz on the open strings through hammer-ons and pull offs.

Faucher's earlier suggestion about 'bouncing' in Moraíto's playing can be
fruitfully applied to this composition by Diego del Morao, whose fingers move
freely yet accurately over different parts of the fretboard. Crucially, these movements create only limited tonal or melodic movement – in fact, some of the actual
notes are hardly hearable as they are enveloped by the traces of the guitarist's
fingering and hammering of the strings (see bars 1, 4 and 5 in Figure 9). The
prominence of such physical encounters with the strings in Diego del Morao's
playing does not only add great dynamism to his sound, similar to what I have
previously described as bouncing and balancing but also elevates the exploration
of timbre to a new compositional principle.

---

[25] Diego del Morao performs this falseta in the key of A Phrygian in the aforementioned guitar
workshop on Buscadores Flamencos (see footnote 21). The authorship of this falseta is here
attributed to Manuel Morao.

Figure 9 Diego del Morao's performance of a cadence in a bulería in E Phrygian

3.4 Rhythmic Heritage in the Morao Family

In this section, I have explored the rhythmic playing of three prominent guitarists from the Morao family by looking at a set of interrelated rhythmic discourses and practices. Manuel Morao is commonly viewed as the main contributor to a distinctively rhythmic type of playing in Jerez, a perception to which his own discussions of contratiempo have in no small degree contributed. On a musical level, I have identified forms of weak-beat accentuation and forward propulsion in his playing that illustrate some of the rhythmic features of contratiempo. On the other hand, I have suggested that contratiempo should not only be taken as an analytical category but also as a significant component of a broader discourse about rhythmic heritage in the Morao family. Morao's claims of ownership over contratiempo and his pitching of this style against the rhythmic practices of younger generations emerge out of a series of overlapping factors, such as a sense of pride for his family, community, and generation, as well as by an impulse to assert the cultural authority of Gitanos in the history of flamenco. In other words, in Manuel Morao's discourse, contratiempo may be understood as the outcome of various overlapping lineages and sentiments towards the past and present of rhythmic guitar playing. A similar example of such overlapping identifications can be found in a short YouTube tutorial (linked earlier in footnote 17) by Diego del Morao about alzapúa, a technique that, as I have previously indicated, is practised in a distinctive way by numerous flamenco guitarists from Jerez. In this video, Diego del Morao notes that the archaic way of practising alzapúa is 'very typical of the Jerez guitar style, of my family' ('muy típica del toque de Jerez, de mi familia'). Here, within the same sentence, Del Morao intertwines a distinctive guitar technique with both family identity and a broader guitar tradition in his city. Thus, the exact relations and possible distinctions between these different lineages become unreadable.

In another workshop about the guitar tradition in Jerez, however, Diego del Morao problematises the suggestion that a musical practice or technique can truly belong to one single individual, since, he notes, all flamenco artists learn from each other.[26] Indeed, as Norman Paul Kliman (2020c) has shown in his analysis of different takes on a traditional melodic phrase by various generations of guitarists, including Manuel Morao, the reality of musical composition, transmission, and performance is often shaped by multidirectional forms of influence and innovation (also see Manuel, 2010). It may seem ironic that Diego del Morao appears to acknowledge this fact in the context of an online workshop that prominently inscribes his playing into a clear family lineage, as illustrated by the concept of the 'Morao dynasty' ('la Saga de los Morao') that appears in the main description of the course, as well as by section titles such as 'Diego del Morao's personal closing phrases' ('Cierres personales de Diego del Morao'), 'Traditional closing phrases of the Morao family' ('Cierres tradicionales de los Morao'), or 'Pedal mechanism in Manuel Morao style' ('Mecanismo del pedal estilo Manuel Morao'). Another way of reading this apparent contradiction is to acknowledge the tactical underpinnings of such unofficial heritage discourses. On the one hand, musicians such as Diego del Morao may be aware of the multifarious reality of musical creation and influence, while on the other, they may choose to lay claim to forms of musical ownership and heritage in specific social, pedagogical, or commercial contexts.

To be sure, my analysis of three generations of guitarists from the Morao family reflects a similar tension. To what extent can Diego del Morao's sophisticated explorations of syncopation, timbre, and attack somehow still be seen from the perspective of patrilineal transmission within the Morao family, and thus as an illustration of local or family heritage? While I have shown that there are tangible forms of continuity and influence between the rhythmic, melodic, and technical choices of these musicians, interpreting them univocally as illustrations of a shared rhythmic heritage remains conceptually complex. As exemplified by Diego del Morao's guitar workshop on Buscadores Flamencos, this guitarist also occasionally struggles with the question of nomenclature when discussing his own rhythmic practices. For instance, on two occasions he employs

---

[26] Diego del Morao makes this comment in clip 5.3 of the aforementioned workshop on Buscadores Flamencos (see footnote 21).

anglophone terminology not immediately familiar in flamenco circles to describe his inventive manipulations of timing and timbre: he defines his rather unusual and syncopated uses of footwork as a 'swing' pattern ('lo llevo a swing') (video 3.1) and later compares the muted downward strokes of his right-hand thumb (as illustrated in Figures 8 and 9) with the slap technique of electric bass players (video 5.3). Regardless of the analytical precision that such concepts may have on a musical level, they illustrate how rhythm, rather than being singularly rooted in the guitarist's local heritage, may point in a variety of other geographical and cultural directions. The vocabulary to discuss the rhythmic heritage of the Morao family, like the forward propulsion of their playing, thus reveals itself as inconclusive and open-ended.[27]

4 Morón de la Frontera

4.1 Rhythm and Ancestry in Morón

Morón is a city in the province of Seville that has been home to significant flamenco artists since the inception of the art form. The acclaimed nineteenth-century singer Silverio Franconetti, who created the *cafés cantantes* (venues for the performance of flamenco song), resided in Morón when he was a child (Vázquez García, 2016, 43); and Morón is also the birthplace of the amateur singer El Tenazas, who won the famous Concurso de Cante Jondo (Deep Song Contest) organised by Manuel de Falla and Federico García Lorca in Granada in 1922 (Rina, 2017, 22). Since the second half of the twentieth century, Morón is also commonly associated with a distinctive rhythmic way of playing flamenco guitar. The architect of this local style was Diego del Gastor (1908–1973), who was born in an adjacent village and moved to Morón as a child. Del Gastor was not an eminently virtuosic guitarist. His guitar style draws on relatively simple single-string melodies performed with the thumb – a concept known as playing *a cuerda pelá* – rather than on more complex classical techniques such as tremolo and picado (Rioja, 1995b, 30). Prior to Diego del Gastor, there were a handful of other guitarists in Morón who practised a similar style, such as José María Álvarez, a non-professional guitarist who had studied with the influential

---

[27] While I have no space to develop this argument here, Diego del Morao's terminology evokes (perhaps unintentionally) the oft-ignored connections between flamenco rhythms and Black musical and cultural traditions. In recent years, various scholars have examined the silenced genealogies of African and Afro-Latin traditions from which aspects of flamenco have germinated, including the bulería style, which is considered as a quintessential element in all public and private flamenco performances in Jerez and which, as K. Meira Goldberg notes, crystalised out of an earlier genre known as the *jaleos de Jerez*. Both names, jaleos and bulerías, continues Goldberg, are semantically entangled with notions of uproar, chaos, and 'scandalous racket' (in Spanish, *jaleo* or *bulla*) (2014, 100) that, as this scholar explores, can be seen as figures of Blackness, in the double sense of racial and religious alterity (2019, 7).

Paco Lucena (1859–1898) and who subsequently went on to teach Pepe Mesa and Pepe Naranjo (Álvarez Caballero, 2003, 105; Rioja, 1995c, 157). According to some scholars, Morón's geographical isolation behind a mountain rug enabled these guitarists to hold on to a sober form of playing that would likely not have survived in other parts of Spain, given the increased professionalisation of guitar playing in the country's cultural centres (Álvarez Caballero, 2003, 104; Rioja, 1995d, 161).

Despite Diego del Gastor's relative lack of technical sophistication, scholars and aficionados of what has come to be known as the 'Morón style' have often pointed to his great sense of musical and rhythmic expressivity. On a rhythmic level, the key features of what Joshua Brown calls the 'ethos' of this style are the ample scope for improvisation based on short melodic phrases, the constant search for rhythmic tension, and the ability to arrive at ever-surprising moments of resolution (Álvarez Caballero, 2003, 104–105; Brown, 2014, 40–41; Rioja, 2003, 20–21; Vázquez García, 2016, 228–244). As I have previously noted, musicians can draw on a variety of cultural habits to achieve new rhythmic effects within existing musical structures (Agawu, 2016, 189) and thus establish a strong communicative bond with audiences familiar with such codes. An example that illustrates some of these principles is Diego del Gastor's performance of a soleá in an episode from the aforementioned documentary series *Rito y geografía del cante*, aired on 25 October 1972.[28] In it, the guitarist uses ironic forms of overstatement to perform common chord cycles and melodic motives. The irony is palpable not only in his curious uses of left- and right-hand techniques – such as his exaggerated rotary movements with the right hand before it falls back on the strings – but also in various bodily gestures. Diego del Gastor rocks his head, displaying a deadpan smile that occasionally changes into a wide-eyed expression to add dramatic emphasis to abrupt volume changes; and he casts subtle glances at his befriended listeners, possibly to confirm if his ironies are reaching the desired effect. 'Teasing' stands out here for its ability to establish a strong communicative bond with an intended audience that, as with other forms of comedy and irony, is placed in a role of complicity. In other words, by withholding a moment of resolution slightly longer than usual, or by subtly exaggerating the volume of individual notes and melodies, Diego del Gastor creates incongruities between what is played and what trained listeners would commonly expect, thus opening up a space for surprise and enjoyment within the cumulative processes of musical performance and reception.

---

[28] https://youtu.be/Ti0AvRnVIms?t=1508. The performance of the soleá commences at 23:40 in the episode.

Diego del Gastor's great skill in applying these principles helps explain the wide attention his playing has accrued, as well as the reverential terms in which it has often been described. Scholars and followers of Diego del Gastor have seen the combination of expressivity and simplicity in his playing as a gateway to ancestral and even spiritual values. For instance, the anthropologist and musician Raúl Rodríguez, who co-founded the successful fusion band Son de la Frontera, writes in highly evocative terms about his visits to Morón: he describes the guitar in this local tradition as 'alive, melodious, shamanic' ('un instrumento vivo, cantor, chamánico') and as 'an Excalibur of rhythm' ('una Excalibur del compás') that resembles other string instruments commonly associated with 'enchantment rituals' ('rituales de encantamiento') such as sitar, sarod, and saz (2014, 29–30). In regard to the dynamic between tradition and innovation, Rodríguez notes that improvisation in the Morón guitar style always operates against the backdrop of 'a code that is undoubtedly ancestral' ('un código indudablemente ancestral') (2014, 29–30). Ángel Sody de Rivas and Pedro Luis Vázquez García, in their respective studies about Diego del Gastor's guitar playing, employ a highly similar terminology. Sody de Rivas, citing Vázquez, notes that the repetition of one singular note with no harmonic embellishments in Morón is 'a common procedure also in certain formulas used for enchantment in primitive societies' ('un procedimiento propio también de ciertas fórmulas de encantamiento de pueblos primitivos') (Sody de Rivas, 2004, 18).

From a historical perspective, the association of Diego del Gastor's playing with concepts of authenticity and ancestry is inaccurate. As Eusebio Rioja observes, the earliest exponent of this technique was Paco Lucena, whose playing dates back only a few generations (2003, 18–20). Furthermore, while Diego del Gastor claimed in 1972 that Morón is a 'land of guitarists' ('suelo de guitarristas'), he was preceded by only a few other practitioners of the instrument.[29] As Rioja continues, when compared to the rapid evolution of flamenco guitar playing in the 1960s elsewhere in Spain, Diego del Gastor's style could perhaps better be defined as anachronistic than as authentic (20). Indeed, some of the most virtuosic guitarists from Diego del Gastor's generation have cast doubts on the alleged spiritual reach of his playing. Manolo Sanlúcar, while claiming that on one level Diego's guitar was 'very deep, very profound, almost primitive' ('muy jonda, muy profunda, casi primitiva'), notes in more practical terms that these virtues reflect Del Gastor's ability to put his relatively meagre technical skills to their best possible use (Álvarez Caballero, 2003, 113–114). In a similar vein, Paco de Lucía and Juan Habichuela have observed that Diego del Gastor's playing was highly personal and appealing in some way ('gracioso'), but technically rather limited (114–115).

---

[29] He makes this comment at approximately 22:50 in the aforementioned documentary episode.

The tropes of authenticity and ancestry that have been commonly applied to Diego del Gastor, and to the Morón style more broadly, can be seen as discursive procedures with which this way of playing is constructed as a form of musical heritage. Diego del Gastor's expressivity is thus understood as establishing communitarian bonds not only between musicians and audiences in the present but also between the present and a partially projected ancestral past. To be sure, the application of such tropes to the Morón guitar style can be compared to other similar discursive 'inventions' in the history of flamenco. Timothy Mitchell, for instance, has analysed the current of 'avant-garde primitivism' that shaped perceptions of purity around the 1922 Concurso de Cante Jondo (1994, 160–164); and Francisco Aix Gracia has examined a purist doctrine known as *neojondismo*, which became especially influential among defenders of Gitano flamenco song in the 1950s (2014, 131–313). As Rioja argues (2003, 21–24), the popularisation of Diego del Gastor's style in the 1960s can be seen as a continuation of *neojondismo* – not least since this guitarist was of Roma ethnicity.

In the case of the Morón style, such primitivist terms are reflective not only of the internal dynamics of flamenco discourse but also of broader international developments that have shaped perceptions of this music since the second half of the twentieth century. In the 1960s, the growing hunger in the West for exotic cultures and experiences led to an influx of travellers and aficionados into the city of Morón. This development was partially facilitated by the large-scale investments in Spain's tourism industry with which the regime of dictator Francisco Franco (1939–1975) aimed to kick-start its backward economy (Balfour, 2000; Crumbaugh, 2009). It was also during this time that the American musician Donn E. Pohren, after being briefly employed as an accountant at an American airbase in Morón, fell in love with Diego del Gastor's guitar playing and decided to establish himself in the city (Vázquez García, 2016, 170). In 1965, Pohren bought an old farmhouse on the outskirts of Morón and converted it into a residence for foreign visitors who came to Andalusia to learn flamenco. Many members of Pohren's clientele had already been introduced to flamenco in the United States by Spanish artists who had gone into exile during and after the Spanish Civil War (1936–1939) (Rina, 2017, 6). Pohren was able to further nurture their appetite for an authentic flamenco experience by writing several books, such as *The Art of Flamenco* (1962), *Lives and Legends of Flamenco* (1964), and *A Way of Life* (1980). The fact that Diego del Gastor was a rather eccentric Gitano performer further stimulated his associations with a special 'pre-modern' aura by Pohren and his young, mostly left-wing, audiences (Rina, 2017, 7; Rioja, 2003, 8–9).

While some foreign visitors merely went to Morón in search of a brief exotic sojourn, others spent much longer periods in the city. Apart from Pohren, various accomplished flamenco scholars and guitarists from the United States, such as Steve Kahn, Evan Harrar, and David Serva, studied extensively with Diego del Gastor. They became the latter's disciples, and subsequently, his most passionate ambassadors abroad. After returning to the United States, many of these guitarists made their careers cultivating and disseminating their knowledge of Diego del Gastor's style in performances, recordings, and other settings. As Joshua Brown has shown, these guitarists' first-hand knowledge of the Morón style even allowed them to teach younger generations of players from Diego del Gastor's own family (2014, 65). In recent years, the contributions that Pohren, Kahn, and others have made to the Morón style have received some institutional acknowledgement in the city of Morón as well. For instance, both Pohren and Kahn have their own webpages on the online portal of Morón's tourism office, alongside other local flamenco artists.[30] Kahn's collection of pictures from his time in Morón, moreover, has been bundled under the title *Flamenco Project* and has been exhibited throughout Andalusia.[31] At the time of writing, there are plans to build a Municipal Flamenco Centre in Morón that will house Kahn's photography collection on a permanent basis.[32]

4.2 Dani de Morón, Rhythm, and Place

While the Morón guitar style is frequently associated with concepts and values that recur to the past, such as ancestry, authenticity, and spiritual essences, this style's local and, according to some, anachronistic character could not have been maintained without the contributions of important international performers, scholars, and aficionados. On the following pages, I will explore how this international imaginary about the Morón style is negotiated both discursively and musically by one of the city's most successful young flamenco guitarists. Daniel López Vicente (born 1981), who operates under the artistic name of Dani de Morón, has positioned himself in recent years among the most successful flamenco soloists, as well as being in high demand as a producer, composer, occasional teacher, and accompaniment guitarist for eminent flamenco dancers and singers. Thus, his work is a privileged site to explore how the rhythmic heritage associated with Diego del Gastor, and with the city of Morón more broadly, is inscribed with new meanings today. I will start by discussing aspects

---

[30] See www.turismomoron.es/es/descubre-moron/flamenco/donn-e-pohren and www.turismo moron.es/es/descubre-moron/flamenco/steve-khan.

[31] A sample of the exhibition can be found here: www.ayto-morondelafrontera.org/opencms/ export/sites/default/morondelafrontera/galeria/download/flamenco_project_catalogo_exposi cion1594634995329.pdf.

[32] www.turismomoron.es/es/descubre-moron/flamenco/puntos-de-interes-flamenco-en-moron/cen tro-municipal-de-flamenco.

of Dani de Morón's poetics and pedagogy of the flamenco guitar, which I then use as a framework for the analysis of his playing.

Like Diego del Morao, whose work I examined in Section 3, Dani de Morón has delivered an online guitar workshop on the website Buscadores Flamencos that unpacks the local dynamics of flamenco guitar playing. In a course entitled 'El toque barbero', an informal term commonly used to describe the guitar style in Morón, Dani de Morón covers a variety of its historical, technical, and rhythmic aspects.[33] In subtle ways, Dani de Morón also invites his viewers to think critically about place-based concepts of rhythm that have shaped perceptions of this style. For instance, in the third video of the course, the guitarist observes that subtle variations in right-hand technique can immediately evoke a strong sense of locality, even if they are audible only briefly: 'it is interesting how one rasgueo, or half a bar, can put you in a certain place' (2:51). However, as he suggests, the 'place' alluded to here should not necessarily be called 'Morón'. Rather than considering Diego del Gastor's style as a reflection of the unique rhythmic atmosphere of his hometown, Dani de Morón prefers to highlight the former's strong personality and musical inventiveness over his ethnicity or relation to a certain birthplace or homeland (*tierra* in Spanish). When thinking about the idiosyncrasies of Diego del Gastor and other players, Dani de Morón observes: 'those personalities are more important to me than where they are from' ('Voy más a esas personalidades que a la tierra') (3:23).

In the fourteenth video, Dani de Morón goes on to analyse Diego del Gastor's style as a rich repertoire of technical and rhythmic elements that are applicable in other musical contexts not immediately associated with Morón. In his discussion of different ways to create rhythmic pulsation in the *tangos*, a 4/4 style, the musician highlights how specific variations in right-hand technique – especially the repetitive use and relatively strong attack of the right-hand index finger to accentuate the weak beats – are a unique driving force in the playing of many guitarists from Morón. While this technique is not commonly applied in other local varieties of tangos, Dani de Morón emphasises that its correct application says little about the locality with which it is frequently associated, or about the identity of the performer. Strictly speaking, performing this type of rhythmic pulsation is exclusively dependent on the right combination of volume, technique, and rhythmic accuracy: 'it's more to do with the way of playing than with the style or the person who plays' (2:30).[34]

---

[33] These videos can be found here: https://buscadoresflamencos.com/producto/toque-de-moron/

[34] In an interview with Fernando González-Caballos, Dani de Morón makes a highly similar claim about the way that the Morón style is more dependent on types of pulsation than on the

To be sure, the full theoretical potential of Dani de Morón's comments remains unexplored in these videos. This may partially be a consequence of the format of course, which is presented as a series of short modules, thus leaving little room for an in-depth analysis of more complex cultural or pedagogical issues. However, based on my analysis of this material, I propose that Dani de Morón's poetics of the flamenco guitar moves away from the place-based concept of heritage that informs most discourses about the Morón style. While, on one level, the artistic name of this guitarist situates him firmly within this tradition, his poetics and pedagogy of the instrument gesture towards a more open-ended understanding of music's expressive qualities. In that sense, his observations are reminiscent of the work of musicologist Siv B. Lie about the entanglements between technique, rhythmic sensitivity, and ethnic belonging in *manouche* guitar playing in France. According to some of Lie's informants, a guitarist's ethnic (Roma) background can be deducted from specific sonic elements in their playing, such as 'specific chord voicings and finger positions, ways of phrasing passages, rhythmic sensibilities, the "attack" of the guitar stroke, and most importantly, the ever-ineffable "feeling" or "heart" that non-Manouches seem to lack' (2017, 103). However, as Lie argues, ethnicity is ultimately an unreliable parameter for the perception of sound (104). Certainly, listeners who are familiar with a musical genre may have credible arguments to identify varying levels of musical and rhythmic skill as well as differences in attack, pulsation, or sonic texture. To recall the discussion about Manuel Morao in Section 3, this guitarist's distinction between elusive rhythmic concepts such as contratiempo and soniquete can be buttressed by real musical criteria, based on Morao's profound understanding of flamenco rhythm and guitar accompaniment. However, as Lie suggest, the perception of such musical features through a framework of ethnicity – a process that she theorises as 'sonic Manoucheness' – may ultimately reveal more about the imaginaries that shape musical perception than about the music itself (104).

Lie's analysis resonates with Dani de Morón's discussion of rhythmic pulsation beyond traditional concepts of place. This musician's pedagogical material contains a subtle invitation to rethink Morón's guitar tradition as a collection of musical 'codes', as he explains in the seventeenth video of the series, that are open and accessible to all. In his view, a level of consistency in the application of such codes is always required. However, he adds, the main purpose of their usage is to push certain forms of flamenco dance and song into a particular emotional direction, rather than to affirm a pre-existing sense of ethnic or

---

performance of specific melodic motives or compositions by Diego del Gastor. Here, he also critiques common associations of this style with purity and authenticity (qtd. Rioja, 2003, 3).

geographical identity. Similarly, as he notes in the same video, different rhythmic codes can trigger surprising and refreshing perceptions in the listener, moving them to a 'different place' ('otro sitio') than they might have initially expected. Thus, pulsation and other rhythmic skills that are commonly inscribed into the heritage of the city of Morón emerge here as an open-ended collection of musical concepts that can propel one onto a journey towards other places.

4.3 Towards Other Places

The pedagogical principles that underpin Dani de Morón's online guitar workshop can be a stimulating way of exploring how this guitarist negotiates concepts of rhythm and heritage in his own playing. Based on the previous discussion, then, I aim to show here that Dani de Morón builds systematically on the 'codes' commonly associated with the style of his hometown but also creatively embeds those elements within a varied collection of rhythmic, harmonic, and compositional structures. Occasionally, the guitarist establishes clear connections with the Morón style through a type of citational practice, where he reproduces and actualises short melodic phrases popularised by Diego del Gastor. For instance, in a soleá named 'Siete Revueltas' (*Cambio de sentido*, 2012), he reproduces two traditional falsetas that were also performed by Diego del Gastor in the episode from *Rito y geografía del cante* that I briefly examined on earlier pages. The first of these is structured as an arpeggio over an F chord (performed by Diego del Gastor at 24:24 in the documentary and by Dani de Morón at 4:00 in 'Siete Revueltas'), while the second is performed as a single-string melody on the third and fourth strings that move from F to E Phrygian (performed by Diego del Gastor at 25:26 in the documentary and by Dani de Morón at 4:16 in his composition).

Beyond such occasional references, Dani de Morón elaborates a deeper performative principle that scholars have associated with his hometown: namely, the way that melodic phrases are enveloped by rhythmic strumming passages known as paseos. When accompanying flamenco song, guitarists tend to employ such strumming passages to give the singer an opportunity to rest between the verses. In solo guitar performances, on the other hand, paseos usually mark a transition between different melodic parts or falsetas. Beyond their functionality as musical interludes, the eminent flamenco guitarist and pedagogue Manolo Sanlúcar has argued that these strumming passages reflect important thematic content of each flamenco style and need to be performed to facilitate the latter's recognisability (2005, 60–62). Today, as Sanlúcar observes, flamenco guitarists appear to be less concerned with the clear exposition of such thematic content: 'Guitarists strum less and less' ('Cada vez se rasguea menos') (61). In this way, Sanlúcar points towards the important role of these contextual passages in preserving what, in his view, is an essential aspect of flamenco's sedimented meanings.

This discussion is of particular relevance for the Morón style where, as scholars have noted, paseos are far from stock elements meant to provide a recognisable background for falsetas (also see Jiménez de Cisneros, 2015, 265–285). According to Evan Harrar, guitarist and connoisseur of the Morón style, '[t]he rhythm dominates, not the falsetas [. . ..] A falseta is only as expressive as the rhythm that precedes and follows it' (No year, no page). Other scholars of the Morón style have defined falsetas as building blocks that can be woven in creative ways into a broader rhythmic context. According to some, the fact that Diego del Gastor's falsetas were rather brief and simple is precisely what allowed this guitarist to interrupt them at unexpected places, thus achieving surprising interactions between the melodies and their rhythmic context (Álvarez Caballero, 2003, 105; Vázquez García, 2016, 231–232).

When playing soleares, guitarists normally perform the paseo as one or two cycles of twelve beats each. In the first cycle, guitarists strum rhythmically over the chords of F, C, and F before resolving to E Phrygian. Here, rasgueo patterns tend to be combined with thumb techniques and soundboard percussion in the run-up to the resolution to the tonic on beat ten, followed by a further metrical accent on beat twelve. In the second cycle, this chord sequence is repeated, but now guitarists tend to use more ornate combinations of arpeggios and legatos, as illustrated in Figure 10.

In two recordings of soleares included on his albums *Cambio de sentido* (2012) and *El sonido de mi libertad* (2015), Dani de Morón manipulates the traditional elements of the paseo by altering their conventional location within the style's metrical structure. In 'Siete Revueltas' (0:57–1:30), while the main components of the paseo are not fundamentally altered, he belatedly introduces an arpeggio in the second cycle. While normally performed between beats one

Figure 10 A common paseo in soleares

and three, the guitarist here not only shortens the arpeggio but also starts it immediately after beat three (bar 9 in Figure 11) and subsequently accelerates it to still enable a resolution of the melody on beat ten (bar 12).

In 'Fe' (2:29), the guitarist introduces a sudden break halfway through the paseo, followed by a syncopated accent on the guitar soundboard and, subsequently, the start of a new melody. Here, the interruption of the paseo illustrates that this guitarist centres his compositional efforts not exclusively on complex melodic variations that remain separated from their rhythmic context; he also searches for rhythmic tension when transitioning between paseos and falsetas.

An extended solo that epitomises many of the aforementioned aspects can be heard on 'A José de la Tomasa', a combination of the song styles of soleares and *cañas* that features on the album *Tardo antiguo* (2020) by flamenco singer Antonio Campos (3:33–4:38).[35] The solo starts as soon as the guitarist takes over from the singer (3:34) and performs a series of downward strokes over an E chord, some of them on the weak beats in the timeline. As illustrated in Figure 12, rather than accentuating beats three, six, eight, and ten, as is common in soleares (see Section 2.1), Dani de Morón accentuates beats four, six, eight, and nine, with a final break on beat eleven.

Figure 11 Rhythmic displacement and condensation of an arpeggio in a paseo on 'Siete Revueltas' (0:57–1:30)

---

[35] A slightly different version of the same solo features on Dani de Morón's 'Camino, verdad y vida' (*Creer para ver*, 2020) (2:24–3:12).

Figure 12 Cadence marking the start of a falseta on 'A José de la Tomasa' (3:33–3:39)

Subsequently, Dani de Morón introduces the falseta. Through copious uses of left-hand legatos and right-hand arpeggios, he creates streams of notes that move fluidly over and between the strong beats. After moving into a D/F chord, he then initiates a chord cycle (D7 – G – C7 – F) commonly used to mark the melodic progression of a sung verse towards the dominant chord (F) and, finally, its resolution to the tonic (E). However, by accelerating these chord changes the guitarist manages to complete the whole sequence in less than seconds. Further rhythmic tension emerges when the guitarist moves into an F chord and then uses a thumb technique to resolve to the tonic just before beat twelve. In the repetition of this melody (3:55), he moves even more daringly through the metrical framework provided by the percussionists. His playing relies extensively on rhythmic acceleration and delay, and the introduction of a momentary harmonic detour into an E major chord (3:59) adds further complexity to his sound. Underneath these cascading flows of melodic phrases, the percussionists perform the strong beats with *nudillos* (rhythmic uses of the knuckles) even though these accents are often not marked on the guitar. The clearest illustration of this dynamic occurs at the end of the solo, where the guitarist moves back into the traditional structure of the paseo. In the final cycle (bar 7 in Figure 13), he performs a syncopated accent on the eight-and-half, thus building tension towards the moment of resolution on beat ten, which is performed by the percussionists but left unstated by the guitar. The fact that, as Leonard Meyer observes, even 'silence may be accented' (1956, 104) is illustrated by the generous *olé* of the percussionists on beat twelve, a rhythmic vocalisation that releases the energy engendered by Dani de Morón's anticipated rhythmic accent and subsequent 'muting' of the cadence.

Such moments of displaced accentuation, acceleration, and condensation can be described as what Dylon Robbins, in his analysis of popular music from Brazil, names 'asymmetrical phrasing', which is a type of rhythmic playing whereby 'a melodic or harmonic structure may resolve at unexpected junctures within a song form, stretching musical phrases beyond the bar lines separating symmetrical groups of measures' (2015, 89). Robbins takes this concept from

Figure 13 Final cadence in the solo on 'A José de la Tomasa' (4:27–4:38)

the work of musicologist Mário de Andrade, who in his *Ensaio sobre a música brasileira* (1928) discusses asymmetrical phrasing as a fundamental component of Brazilian popular song. For Andrade, asymmetrical phrasing is not an example of syncopation or polyrhythm, but rather an aspect of the prosody of sung poetry, motivated by the vocal constraints of the singer (Andrade, 1972, 29–39). To be sure, in the case of flamenco guitar playing, there are no immediate physical constraints – such as the need to breathe – that force a musician to resolve a phrase at an unexpected point within a cycle. Nevertheless, based on Robbins's discussion, I would like to suggest an inverse interpretation of asymmetrical phrasing: namely, that it is irregular timing that engenders a state of heightened bodily effort rather than being caused by it. In other words, asymmetrical phrasing illustrates how rhythm affects the musician's body and, to borrow Pierre Sauvanet's expression, possesses it (2000, 132–138). Dani de Morón is a guitarist who unapologetically externalises such traces of bodily effort and tension in his recordings and performances. A clear example can be found on his composition 'Fe' (3:04), already discussed in this section, when the guitarist concludes a protracted variation over the chord progression F – G – F. Interestingly, the true moment of rhythmic release here exceeds the twelve-beat cycle and falls between beats three and four of the next cycle, where the guitarist inaugurates a new paseo. Notably, this release of rhythmic tension becomes audible not only through the staccato attack with which he performs the F chord but also through an emphatic sigh (3:04). This is yet another illustration of the fluid connections established between falsetas, paseos, and their associated energies in Dani de Morón's music. Rather than following a stable dynamic where falsetas reflect a state of heightened effort while paseos are meant for rest and relief, his playing builds and releases rhythmic energy across such structural boundaries.[36]

On earlier pages, I have identified the search for rhythmic tension, weak-beat accentuation, and surprising resolutions as recurrent features in Dani de Morón's playing. Since scholars have identified that such rhythmic principles are guiding aspects of the Morón style, their presence in Dani de Morón's playing 'might suggest that this musician draws in highly elaborate ways on the rhythmic heritage of his hometown. Dani de Morón's performances of rhythm, in that sense, could be seen as an innovative yet ultimately recognisable performance of local heritage. On another level, and to recall Dani de Morón's pedagogical discussion that I explored on earlier pages, perhaps his personal creativity and rhythmic playfulness should not be inscribed too easily into a pre-available repertoire of rhythmic and compositional pathways. Rather, the elements commonly identified with the Morón style provide the building blocks that support this musician's search for open-ended forms of rhythmic creativity. This dynamic is perhaps best exemplified on the title track of his debut album *Cambio de sentido* ('Change of direction'). The recording is an eloquent exploration of rhythm, harmony, and polyphony as it contains two intersecting guitars floating in and out of lead and accompaniment roles. The track starts in a D# Phrygian key, where both guitars develop an evocative melody consisting of short phrases that are smoothly connected through legatos. Midway through the composition, while no modulation takes place, the harmonic atmosphere of the track subtly changes from D# Phrygian to E Phrygian (2:22), an effect that has likely been achieved in the studio by switching the position of the capo of one of the guitars. This change inaugurates two falsetas that bear a much stronger resemblance than the first section to the types of pulsation, technique, and melodic phrasing commonly employed in the Morón style. For instance, in this new section, the guitarist introduces abundant legatos and hammer-ons to create long, cascading strains of notes, followed by punchy attacks with the right-hand thumb, as well as moments of resolution on weak beats in the timeline (2:54–3:12).

Beyond its potential reference to this change in musical atmosphere, I read the 'change of direction' alluded to in the track's title as a broader poetic statement. Crucially, the guitarist does not move from a recognisable and traditional musical atmosphere towards a more modern-sounding exploration of harmony and melody, which might symbolise a search for innovation based

---

[36] Such externalisations of bodily effort appear even more systematically on his solo album *Creer para ver* (2020), such as on the bulería 'La Mazaroca' (4:00) and at the end of the soleá 'Camino, verdad y vida' (5:45). Due to their prominence in his recordings and performances, I suspect that such bodily signs are not merely incidental expressions of the guitarist's mental concepts of rhythm but are meant to support what might be called a poetics of embodied playing.

on a firm statement of the importance of tradition. Rather, by moving away from modern-sounding melodies and harmonies (as reflected by the key of D# Phrygian) to the more traditional sound of E Phrygian, the guitarist also infuses the 'codes' associated with the Morón style with new poetic meaning. In other words, this transition between different harmonic, melodic, and rhythmic atmospheres should perhaps not be interpreted as a return to a fixed point of departure, but rather as a change of direction that aims to free such apparently recognisable elements from previous place-based connotations. In Dani de Morón's solo performance of this piece at the Círculo Flamenco de Madrid in 2015, the transition between both sections is marked in an even more emphatic manner.[37] In a way similar to the recording, he starts the piece by developing the main theme in D# Phrygian. However, to achieve the same change of harmonic environment, the guitarist now modulates into E Phrygian (3:42). This change is further marked by the fact that he slows down the tempo, changes his foot accompaniment, and makes more copious uses of soundboard percussion and punchy thumb passages on the bass strings. The audience responds enthusiastically to this transition, shown by the fact that their muted jaleos make place for more energetic exclamations after the modulation. Like in most genres, flamenco audiences tend to appreciate recognisable elements in a performance, especially when such elements are culturally overdetermined by concepts of tradition and locality (also see Section 5.2). But perhaps, Dani de Morón employs those factors of recognisability not merely to please the audience, or to reaffirm his personal affiliations with the artistic heritage of his hometown. Instead, the compositional structure of 'Cambio de sentido' suggests that these elements from Morón's musical heritage can also inform a forward-looking exploration of other places and directions.

5 Rhythm and Heritage across Borders: Falseta Virus

5.1 Musical Activity in the Covid-19 Pandemic

In early 2020, when the world came to a sudden standstill due to the Covid-19 pandemic, social media gained an unprecedented role in channelling musical activity around the globe. Like most other musicians, flamenco guitarists quickly turned to online platforms to share concerts, lessons, and other content. In the final section of this Element, I will analyse an online guitar contest organised in the early months of the pandemic by the flamenco guitar store Solera Flamenca, based near Barcelona. According to the organisers, this contest was meant as a strictly friendly initiative to support the global community of flamenco

---

[37] A recording of this performance can be found here: www.youtube.com/watch?v=AV_cW2fFDug.

guitarists, many of which were left without public fora to play and teach.[38] The contest, appropriately titled 'Falseta Virus', invited participants to submit their personal take on a well-known composition by Diego del Gastor, whose work I have discussed in the previous section. Participants were divided into a professional and a non-professional category. A jury, comprised of staff from Solera Flamenca and other professionals of the flamenco guitar industry, evaluated the first group of submissions, whereas the recordings in the professional category were submitted to a popular vote carried out via email. The winners in both categories were awarded a hand-crafted flamenco guitar.

Due to the large number of professional and non-professional guitarists that participated in Falseta Virus (180 submissions in total), this competition provides an interesting opportunity to explore how concepts of rhythm in flamenco guitar are evolving in the current global mediasphere. On the following pages, I will firstly examine how guitarists have reworked key rhythmic components of the original falseta. Thereafter, I will discuss a series of online reactions to Falseta Virus. I will situate these comments within a series of broader developments in flamenco culture, such as the increasingly transnational and digital circulation of musical performances and pedagogies. More broadly, I use Falseta Virus as a case study to explore how concepts of rhythmic heritage are evolving in transnational and digital contexts.

A brief description of the basic rules of Falseta Virus seems in order. Firstly, participants were given fourteen days to submit their recordings after the competition was launched. Due to this limited time frame, as well as the strict social-distancing measures that were in place in almost all countries at the time (March and April 2020), participants had to rely on the most immediate forms of musical creativity at their disposal. On the other hand, the organisers did not prescribe a specific format or maximum length for the submissions. Indeed, a cursory glance at the material reveals that most submissions were recorded in a rather casual manner on a smartphone. Only a few guitarists submitted multi-track recordings made in a home studio, including one submission where a guitarist is shown on different screens playing different instruments – a feature of online music-making that became popular under Covid-19 due to prevalent social restrictions.[39]

Before launching Falseta Virus in April 2020, Solera Flamenca already had a strong online presence. One of its most successful promotion strategies are the frequent releases of high-quality videos on YouTube with acclaimed flamenco guitarists performing short pieces on one of the hand-crafted guitars

---

[38] Personal communication by Jordi Franco, co-owner of Solera Flamenca, 15 June 2023.
[39] See the submissions by Yerai Cortés (www.youtube.com/watch?v=ICcJ1U8xNEM) and Manuel Urbina (www.youtube.com/watch?v=DxR8u8JZ6II).

that are for sale. Over the years, these recorded performances have evolved from mere promotional material into an influential online archive of cutting-edge guitar playing. Falseta Virus, then, can be seen as another successful online activity with which Solera Flamenca has contributed to a growing archive of modern practices of flamenco guitar. As such, the store has attained an important role in mediating contemporary perceptions and imaginaries around the instrument.[40]

While there is a vast body of scholarship on the role of digital platforms in shaping musical practices across the globe (see, among others, Hesmondhalgh et al., 2023; McDowell, 2015; Tan, 2019), this topic has thus far received limited attention in flamenco scholarship. One notable exception is the essay 'The New Flamenco School Show: Breaking Stereotypes and Planting Seeds of Discourse on Race' by flamenco dancer and pedagogue Julie Galle Baggenstoss. In it, Galle Baggenstoss discusses how online environments are impacting on the perceptions of flamenco held by recent generations of students in the United States. For members of Generation Z, writes Galle Baggenstoss, flamenco is part of a new 'imaginative geography'[41] (2022, 432) that revolves much more around online communities than around physical locations in Andalusia, or Spain more broadly. The online interactions of young flamenco practitioners, she notes, range from 'viewing appropriated symbols of cultural expression, to passively viewing amateur videos on social media, to actively chatting with peers [in] closed discussion groups of international students who share common interests' (2022, 432). While the participants in Falseta Virus, and Solera Flamenca's clientele more broadly, are not part of one single generation, Galle Baggenstoss's discussion brings to the fore how online interactions are creating new perceptions of place, identity, and community in flamenco culture. This suggestion seems especially relevant in the context of the global pandemic, when many 'offline' contexts of sociality became suddenly unavailable. During this time, Falseta Virus provided participants with a distraction from the lockdown and thus contributed to the emergence of online networks of care – a concept that is echoed by emergent scholarship on the value of music as a coping mechanism during the Covid-19 pandemic (Agamennone, Palma & Sarno, 2022). Since Covid-19, musical practices and pedagogies have been operating more and more at the intersection of online and offline contexts. As I aim to demonstrate on the following pages, these developments are also impacting on practices and perceptions of rhythm in modern flamenco guitar.

---

[40] At the time of writing, Solera Flamenca's YouTube channel has approximately 45,000 followers.

[41] Galle Baggenstoss borrows this term from Edward Said's *Orientalism* (1978).

5.2 The Zarzamora Lick

As already stated, all participants of Falseta Virus were given the same task: to record a short video with their personal interpretation of a falseta generally attributed to Diego del Gastor and popularly known as the 'Zarzamora lick', due to its melodic resemblance to the 1946 copla song 'La Zarzamora' ('The Blackberry') (Brown, 2014, 83).[42] Set in the key of A major, the falseta starts as a single-string melody performed with the index and middle finger of the right hand, a technique known as *picado*. Diego del Gastor created a strong rhythmic context for portions of the melody by enveloping them with strumming passages over the tonic and its dominant (E7).[43] After a series of initial melodic variations over A major and E7, the melody then moves towards the chord of D major, followed by a sequence of descending phrases over E7 that run from the higher strings towards the bass strings. In Diego del Gastor's original rendering, these descending phrases were connected through copious pull offs, a technique with which the guitarist would build tension before the final resolution to the tonic. In one famous live performance, which was also used as the basis for Falseta Virus, Diego del Gastor teasingly applies rubato in one final upward movement of the melody prior to the cadence. Subsequently, he picks up the original speed and resolves to the tonic.

As Joshua Brown notes, 'this playful melodic line invariably stirs up audiences, inciting shouts of "¡Viva Morón!" ("Long live Morón!"), "¡Diego!" and "¡Olé!"' (2014, 83). Indeed, the falseta contains various rhythmic and technical features commonly associated with the Morón guitar style, such as an emphasis on single-string melodic lines, the teasing use of left-hand slides, volume changes to create effects of under- and overstatement and the dazzling repetition of brief melodic phrases to create tension before the cadence. Today, the Zarzamora lick can be heard in informal performances of flamenco guitar outside Morón as well. Flamenco guitarists quickly learn to incorporate it into their repertoire, not only because it is technically undemanding but also because it is easily recognised by audiences and represents a form of traditional playing that tends to be successful among aficionados. In that sense, performances of this falseta can be seen as an informal heritage practice in flamenco. Not only do such performances affirm the ongoing value of a type of guitar playing that, as I explored in Section 4, is commonly associated with ancestry and authenticity

---

[42] Diego del Gastor's performance of the falseta can be viewed here: www.youtube.com/watch?v=PSBcmHooNKc. It is unclear whether the guitarist took the melody directly from 'La Zarzamora'. Brown names the 1930 flamenco song 'Guajiras cómicas' ('Comical *guajiras*') as another possible source (2014, 83–84).

[43] For more information about the dynamic between rhythm and melody in Diego del Gastor's playing, also see Section 4.

but they also help affirm a cultural bond between musicians and their audiences around a shared appreciation for the traditional repertoire. To be sure, the aim of Falseta Virus was not to invite guitarists to reproduce the Zarzamora lick as faithfully as possible or to contribute in any way to its curation and preservation. Nevertheless, the diverse set of renderings that it has given rise to is an apt starting point to explore how modern flamenco guitarists negotiate the dynamic between preservation and innovation in their playing.

For contemporary audiences, the Zarzamora lick may not only conjure up associations with Diego del Gastor, Morón, and traditional guitar playing but also with the music of the fusion band Pata Negra, who included a blues-inspired variation of the same melody on 'Blues de la Frontera', the title track from their 1987 album. As Joshua Brown argues, Pata Negra's music has inspired a younger generation of Andalusian artists – most significantly, the band Son de la Frontera – to search for innovative combinations of traditional flamenco with other musical genres, including Afro-Cuban sounds (2014, 72–79). Importantly, the two groups that I have mentioned here have adopted the word *frontera* ('border'), originally part of Morón's toponym, for the names of their album (*Blues de la frontera*) and band name (Son de la Frontera). This illustrates how the city of Morón is part of a broader musical imaginary where it does not only connote ancestry and authenticity but also forms of musical and cultural border-crossing. It thus seems appropriate that the Zarzamora lick was chosen for an online contest organised during a global pandemic, when digital sociality was one of the few ways in which communication across physical and geographical borders could still be established.

5.3 Concepts of Rhythm in Falseta Virus

In my analysis of a selection of reworkings of the Zarzamora lick, I will focus on two key rhythmic elements. Firstly, I will examine the way that guitarists envelop the main melody with a wider rhythmic context. I have chosen this criterion due to the importance that is generally awarded to rhythmic context in the Morón guitar style, as I explored in Section 4. Secondly, I will examine how several contestants performed the second part of the falseta which consists of various descending phrases in the build-up of rhythmic tension before the cadence. This criterion also builds on Section 4, where I examined how the search for surprising resolutions is an important rhythmic principle in the Morón guitar style.[44]

In Diego del Gastor's original rendering of the falseta, the rhythmic context for the melody is established through three recurring techniques: up-and-down

---

[44] In the following analysis, I have selected relevant examples from the submissions of forty-two professional guitarists and twelve finalists in the amateur category, which can all be viewed on YouTube. Links have been included where relevant.

movements of the right-hand index finger, rasgueos, and soundboard taps (see, for instance, bars 8 until 12 in Figure 14). In previous sections, I have discussed how subtle differences in such uses of technique and accentuation in flamenco guitar playing bear significant cultural meaning, as they shape broader identifications with specific traditions and localities. As a cursory look at the submissions for Falseta Virus reveals, most guitarists have employed a much wider repertoire of techniques and accentuation patterns than Diego del Gastor. Two professional guitarists who visibly indulge in the evocation of a strong percussive context for their variations on the Zarzamora lick are Paco Fernández and

Figure 14 Diego del Gastor's Zarzamora lick

Figure 14 (cont)

Jerónimo Maya.[45] Both guitarists playfully combine a variety of percussive effects through strumming, punchy attacks with the right-hand thumb, harmonics, and soundboard tapping. Their submissions illustrate how the development of

---

[45] Paco Fernández: www.youtube.com/watch?v=5fznOy7jt7M. Jerónimo Maya: www.youtube.com/watch?v=ssRKsn0F0hQ.

a rhythmic framework for the subsequent development of melodic variations is a process that, in itself, can be worthy of experimentation. In opposition to Fernández and Maya, the winner in the professional category, Didi Boado, makes much more limited use of soundboard percussion. Instead, his pulsation relies heavily on hammer-ons performed with the left hand and on short explosive rasgueos flicked from behind the right-hand thumb.[46] In one of the online comments, one viewer goes as far as to suggest that Boado's performance sounds 'as if the Morón style has made a detour to Cádiz' ('como Morón pasado por Cádiz').[47] This viewer's interpretation is likely motivated by the up-beat tempo and major harmonies that feature prominently in Boado's playing, and which flamenco aficionados will normally associate with the playful rhythms of the *bulería de Cádiz*. The winner in the amateur category, Kojiro Tokunaga, is another guitarist who has combined different techniques and accentuation patterns.[48] Initially, he reproduces Diego del Gastor's pulsation by using a recurrent set of soundboard taps that broadly correspond with common accentuation patterns in the bulería de Morón (see Figure 1). Later, however, Tokunaga introduces a series of new techniques and melodic motives with which he substitutes a strumming passage over E7 (bars 8–12 in Figure 14): he flicks his fingers from behind the thumb and then performs a short melody with the right-hand thumb, followed by syncopated soundboard percussion and an explosive rasgueo to mark the transition towards the next portion of the main melody (0:13–0:15). Tokunaga's rich exploration of syncopation and timbre in this passage is not immediately reminiscent of Diego del Gastor and has a much clearer antecedent in the work of Diego del Morao, who competed in the professional category of Falseta Virus.[49] When viewed alongside the recording by Tokunaga, Diego del Morao's submission provides an even more daunting example of syncopation, where the strong beats are often only hinted at through a combination of off-beat resolutions of the melody, and crucially, through one of this guitarist's signatures: the end of the cadence on beat ten is left unstated on the guitar but performed with a nod of the head and an upward swing of the guitarist's body.[50]

As shown by these different recordings, those portions of the Zarzamora lick that were originally aimed at providing rhythmic context have now become a point of departure for new explorations of timbre, technique, and syncopation. The fact that

---

[46] www.youtube.com/watch?v=tg9Z2iVJuZo.

[47] This comment can be found under the link included in footnote 46.

[48] www.youtube.com/watch?v=ERqUd9XVmA0.

[49] www.youtube.com/watch?v=nHRmRIfSXII.

[50] Similar forms of syncopated playing that are also partially indebted to Diego del Morao can be viewed in submissions by Pepe Fernández (www.youtube.com/watch?v=IHD1hS5N2hQ) and Luis de Perikin (www.youtube.com/watch?v=K2XVZXrDaes).

several participants directed their creative energies at those contextual passages confirms Manolo Sanlúcar's assessment, discussed in Section 4.3, that contemporary flamenco guitarists are less preoccupied with the evocation of recognisable thematic content than earlier generations of players. Indeed, modern guitarists appear to search for more fluid compositional structures wherein rhythmic pulsation is less prominent. This development is further illustrated in two submissions by Antonio Segura and José Cuesta, who both incorporate the single-string melody from the original composition into a dense musical texture where they alternate between arpeggios, scales, and complex chord voicings.[51] José Cuesta, in particular, switches between different right-hand techniques and thus alters the traditional functions of the thumb, as a driving force for the *a cuerda pelá* style, and strumming, commonly reserved for contextual passages. A submission in the professional category by Rycardo Moreno provides another rich example of this dynamic.[52] Moreno is part of a current generation of guitarists who are fully proficient in both flamenco and jazz. Due to his skilful uses of improvisation, the coordinates of his performance appear to be constantly shifting. He embellishes the main melody with harmonics and appoggiaturas, thus creating new connections between different portions of the falseta. In his playing, moreover, rhythmic strumming is only one component in a much wider constellation of techniques, riffs (short phrases that are rhythmically repeated), and improvised melodies that remain suspended between their leading and secondary functionality.

As I noted in Section 2.1, perceptions of rhythmic tension commonly emerge when musicians employ a recognisable series of cultural habits such as withholding, teasing, and exaggeration. One specific form of rhythmic tension is what I have described earlier as asymmetrical phrasing, where musical phrases are stretched or condensed in such ways that their resolution occurs before or after common reference points within the metrical context. Such forms of asymmetry are present in the work of various guitarists who contributed to Falseta Virus. Some of them have introduced the original composition into alternative metrical structures, which leads to a temporal resignification of the original melody: Paco Soto and Juan Manuel Moreno both perform it as a tangos (a 4/4 measure);[53] Miguel Ángel Cortés repurposes it as a *colombiana*;[54] and Alfredo Mesa has

---

[51] Antonio Segura: www.youtube.com/watch?v=agG-wYTNddU. José Cuesta: www.youtube.com/watch?v=0R5hKjNtjcQ.

[52] www.youtube.com/watch?v=IKciXxNVJ2I.

[53] Paco Soto: www.youtube.com/watch?v=9NrsUi1kucM. Juan Manuel Moreno: www.youtube.com/watch?v=KkLBA1Gq0h8.

[54] Miguel Ángel Cortés: www.youtube.com/shorts/GJaMDPkSreY. The colombiana is a 4/4 rhythm performed in a major key, created in the 1930s by singer Pepe Marchena and inspired by Mexican and Basque folkloric songs. Despite its name, the style has no clear connections with Colombian music and is mostly an exoticist projection of musical energies associated with Latin America (Ordóñez Eslava, 2020, 61–63).

chosen the structure of a *cabales*, a twelve-beat cycle whose accentuation patterns are more similar to the style of *siguiriyas* (see Jiménez de Cisneros, 2015, 113) than bulerías.[55]

Other guitarists, while keeping the overarching structure of the bulería, create asymmetry by shortening or extending designated portions of the melody. To refer once more to Rycardo Moreno, when performing the transition from D to E7 (bars 31–33 in Figure 14 and bars 1–3 in Figure 15), he introduces the descending melody with an arpeggio starting on beat ten. The arpeggio here has the function of an anacrusis as it induces the melody with anticipatory movement (see Butterfield, 2006). Subsequently, Moreno omits one note from the melody that leads to a subtle displacement of the original resolution to the note of C# on beat ten (bar 40 in Figure 14): when transposed to the key of Diego del Gastor's performance, instead of playing F# – E – F# – E – F# – E – F# – E – C#, Moreno shortens it by playing F# – E – F# – E – F# – E – C#.[56] On various occasions, moreover, Moreno duplicates portions of the melody in an alternative form elsewhere on the fretboard (see, especially, 0:30–0:32 and 0:39–0:43), thus suspending the resolutive force of common rest points in the original falseta. One final recording where the resolution of the melody is displaced and therefore somehow undermined can be found is that of guitarist Raúl el Perla.[57] While this guitarist starts the falseta in the key of A major, towards the end, following a long improvisation on a set of downward phrases on the bass strings, he resolves the melody on beat ten at the same time as he switches into the key of A Phrygian by

Figure 15 Rycardo Moreno's performance of a portion of the Zarzamora lick, corresponding with bars 31–40 in Figure 14

---

[55] www.youtube.com/watch?v=xfs7-6kB0Qk.

[56] Rycardo Moreno has recorded the same falseta as part of the composition 'Bordón Gitano' with eminent flamenco guitarist Tomatito (*Concierto No. 1 Guitarra Flamenca: La Perla*, 2024).

[57] www.youtube.com/watch?v=cMj6Bjgu9Vg.

using an emphatic thumb-stroke over the chord of Bb (1:02). Here, the moment of resolution of the previous melody becomes ambiguous, as it coincides with the start of a new phrase over a dominant chord (Bb) belonging to a new harmonic atmosphere. The resolution of the melody, then, does not occur in the key of A major, but rather in A Phrygian.

In sum, the selection of submissions that I have analysed here differ quite radically from the forms of pulsation, improvisation, and rhythmic tension that were present in Diego del Gastor's performance of the Zarzamora lick. Most significantly, various guitarists have departed from one of the most salient features of Diego del Gastor's guitar playing, which I have theorised as the evocation of a recognizable rhythmic pulse – in other words, rhythm understood as a situating, enveloping framework for melody. Most participants keenly switch between different techniques and musical codes; for instance, by alternating between forms of straight, loose, and syncopated timing; by borrowing techniques and harmonies from other genres (classical, jazz, soul, and blues); and by combining traditional melodic passages with varied (and often virtuosic) intersections. To conclude this section, I will explore how this move away from a traditional concept of rhythm can be related to the increasingly transnational dynamics of the flamenco industry, as well as to the recent advent of digital tools and platforms for musical practice.

5.4 Rhythmic Feel in the Global-Digital Age

Kojiro Tokunaga, who won Falseta Virus in the amateur category, was praised in various comments on YouTube for his capacity to convey the 'spirit' and 'flow' of Diego del Gastor's original falseta whilst avoiding unnecessary displays of virtuosity. Such comments include the following: 'Well, there you have those from the homeland (*tierra*) with their virtuosity, and then Kojiro Tokunaga who makes it swing so much that it blows you away'; 'They all play very well ... but they've made it so complex that they've lost the air of Morón ... .'[58] In fact, some viewers were surprised by the fact that Tokunaga competed as an amateur as his musical skills, in their view, surmounted that of many professional players.[59] On a cultural level, the fact that Tokunaga is from Japan did not go unnoticed. Several viewers highlighted that it may be time to revisit traditional hierarchies between flamenco musicians from Spain and abroad: 'Pretty amazing that an Asian guy plays it with more feel than someone

---

[58] The reactions to Tokunaga's submission can be found here: www.youtube.com/watch?v=ERqUd9XVmA0. In my translations, I have edited some uses of punctuation to improve their readability.

[59] Kojiro Tokunaga has a successful flamenco guitar duo with his brother and participates actively in the music industry of Japan.

from Diego del Gastor's homeland (*tierra*)'; '[T]hat an Asian guy shows us how it's done, some just can't accept it'; 'Congratulations boss, for being an amateur champion and for knowing how to appreciate our culture, in this case flamenco, more than many in our own country'.What I find particularly significant about these comments is that some viewers detect a local 'air' or 'feel' in Tokunaga's playing. On earlier pages, I have identified a broad variety of rhythmic practices in the submissions of both Tokunaga and many other participants in Falseta Virus, such as varied explorations of timbre, asymmetrical phrasing, and syncopated timing not commonly associated with the Morón guitar style. Thus, even though different rhythmic practices coexist in Tokunaga's playing, his performance is still appreciated by some viewers as a transmission of the adequate local atmosphere. This leads back to the main question that I began this Element with: how is rhythm constructed as a form of cultural heritage? In the context of Falseta Virus, this initial question sets off another series of questions: what does rhythmic feel mean for flamenco audiences today? To what extent is it (still) mapped onto concepts of the local? And how are appreciations of rhythmic feel impacted by the transnational and online circulation of flamenco?

Admittedly, substantial additional fieldwork among flamenco practitioners and aficionados would be required to answer these questions in full. Nevertheless, based on the examples from Falseta Virus that I have examined in earlier pages, I would like to suggest a few avenues of research that can help illuminate these questions. Due to the circulation of flamenco in increasingly transnational contexts, I argue, the recognition of rhythmic 'air' or 'feel' by global audiences reveals itself as a complex process involving a growing number of musical, cultural, and critical perspectives.

As mentioned in earlier paragraphs, Kojiro Tokunaga's submission has motivated some viewers to comment on the way that musical skill is partially rooted in the cultural identity of a musician. While most viewers express great enthusiasm for this guitarist, some of them also reproduce reductive stereotypes of Spaniards and non-Spaniards and their respective relations to flamenco. One could ask, for instance, whether a musician as skilful as Tokunaga who was born in Spain, rather than in Japan, would ever receive praise for their capacity to, as one viewer puts it in an aforementioned comment, 'appreciate' flamenco – a verb that subtly hints at a persistent border between those who can claim ownership over this music (as reflected by the expression 'our culture' in the same comment) and those who cannot but respectfully approach it from the outside. In reality, the relations of Spaniards with flamenco are also manifold, especially in regions and communities that have had little exposure to it. Levels of appreciation for flamenco are therefore not necessarily higher among

Spaniards than among individuals from elsewhere for whom, due to their background and education, music may already be a crucial way of engaging with the world. The ongoing need to anchor the quality of a performer in their nationality, or in broader cultural and racial categories such as 'Asian', is an indicator of the complex questions over belonging that continue to inform flamenco discourse.[60]

Here, I would like to make a short detour to illustrate that the association between rhythmic feel and cultural identity in flamenco, while reminiscent of the racialised interpretations of rhythm that I discussed in Section 2.2, can be motivated by various reasons. In a series of publications about *cante gitano*, a song repertoire largely based on the contributions of prominent flamenco-performing Roma families, the anthropologist Iván Periáñez has argued that the transmission of song is a profoundly localised process involving the situated memories, knowledges, and lifeworlds of Gitanos. In this context, he suggests that rhythm – or what he dubs 'rhythmic memory' – has both musical and cultural value, as it not only shapes the ways that performers and listeners 'inhabit' the moods associated with specific musical content but also operates as a conduit for cultural memory – specifically, memories of the systemic repression of the Roma since the fifteenth century (2023, 151). Acknowledging such localised meanings of flamenco is necessary, notes Periáñez, since these have often been ignored or, alternatively, converted into reductive stereotypes of Otherness in understandings of flamenco as 'world music' or 'world heritage' (Periáñez, 2016, 30–31).

In one of Periáñez's studies, he evokes the voices of several interlocutors from the Spanish Roma community who support this localised interpretation of the Gitano song repertoire. One of these commentators compares the rhythmic memories of Spanish Roma families to that of other practitioners of flamenco: 'At the end of the day, it's just a matter of having developed certain senses to be able to listen. A Japanese may come and learn it with a metronome and play like

---

[60] The reader interested in further exploring such attitudes towards flamenco musicians from Asia may wish to refer to an interview with the Chinese flamenco guitarist Can Wang on a local television channel in Andalusia, available on the guitarist's YouTube channel: www.youtube .com/watch?v=43mbqOMM2P0. In the interview, before the guitarist is introduced to the viewers in full, the camera zooms in on his hands, thus refraining from showing any bodily features that could reveal his ethnic background. This camera movement occurs at the same time as the presenter verbally prepares the audience for the 'surprise' of seeing an Asian musician perform flamenco guitar. At this stage, she goes as far as to suggest that Can Wang's performance is reminiscent of the Morón style, despite the fact that he is performing a *rondeña*, a solo style not commonly associated with that locality. This example illustrates how questions of cultural and racial difference continue to shape perceptions not only of the performances but also of the *bodies* of flamenco performers (dancers, singers, but also guitarists). For a more detailed consideration of such issues, mainly from the perspective of flamenco dance, see Goldberg, Bennahum, & Heffner Hayes, 2015; Goldberg, 2019; and Márquez, 2022.

a calculator, but he doesn't give it that feel, he doesn't have the rhythm' ('Al final no es otra cosa que tener desarrollaos ciertos sentidos pa poder escuchar. Ahora viene un japonés y aprende, le da el metrónomo, es una calculadora pero no le da el feeling, no tiene ese compás') (qtd. Periáñez, 2016, 39). Clearly, this comment is based on an informal verbal interaction, possibly to foreground a voice rooted in oral culture that does not share in what Shzr Ee Tan names the 'potentially elite language styles of "academese"' (2021, 4). On the other hand, this informant's vindication of rhythm as situated knowledge coexists uncomfortably with an Orientalist stereotype of the 'Japanese'. As Shzr Ee Tan notes, East Asian musicians are often seen as 'passionless technicians and automatons' (2021, 151), a perception that belittles not only the musical skill of Japanese, Asian, and other non-Spanish practitioners of flamenco but also the long and challenging process of deep immersive learning that many of them engage in when spending long periods in Spain to study this music. On one level, then, the commentary of Periáñez's informant iterates a common perception about out-groups in flamenco discourse where, as Joshua Brown notes, '[e]xternal affiliations are often met with distrust and perceived as threats because they symbolize a departure from locally lived histories and modes of expression' (2014, 114).

From a different viewpoint, and in the context of Periáñez's critical discourse, this reference to overtly 'metronomic' forms of rhythmic practice is perhaps not so much meant as a racial slur than as an affirmation of the importance of embodied processes of musical learning. Indeed, the metronome, while widely employed by flamenco musicians today, has historically been at the heart of disputes over embodied and mechanical ways of developing rhythmic skill (Bonus, 2021). While the distinction between rhythmic feel and metronomic learning is thus not necessarily a dichotomy, what is important is that Periáñez's informant perceives it as such. On another level, then, the voice of Periáñez's informant appears to operate as a critical counterpoint to global heritage agendas that have tended to overlook such local dynamics (also see Periáñez, 2019). In this critical context, the emphasis on rhythm as part of a cultural identity, while not unproblematic, can perhaps be better understood as a tactical response to a longer history of cultural dispossession.[61]

To return to Falseta Virus, even flamenco musicians who do have access to local musical knowledge and heritage in Andalusia will have to balance such affiliations with new professional demands. Joshua Brown has shown, for instance, that guitarists from Diego del Gastor's own family are now required to venture beyond the style of their acclaimed forebearer since 'musical versatility

---

[61] To take such critiques of decontextualised approaches to heritage one step further, it may be necessary to also expand concepts of situated and embodied knowledge beyond traditional in-groups in flamenco. I will return to this point in the Conclusion.

and technical wizardry are often preconditions for employment' (2014, 116). Similarly, as Matthew Machin-Autenrieth's fieldwork in the city of Granada reveals, those guitarists who still perform in strongly localised ways are increasingly perceived as representatives of 'an older conception of the flamenco tradition, a way of playing that no longer has a place in the flamenco world' (2017, 164). While this does not mean that concepts of the local are disappearing altogether, Machin-Autenrieth suggest that the local is now mostly maintained on a discursive level rather than corresponding with a tangible musical reality: 'Whether a local guitar style exists at any tangible level, in a sense, is not important. What is important is that some people say it exists – it thus becomes a conduit for expressing musical identity at a local level' (2017, 164). As I have noted at the beginning of this study, musical discourse and practice are always overlapping realities. That said, Machin-Autenrieth's conclusion about the contemporary dynamics of the local can be extended to contemporary perceptions of rhythmic feel. As illustrated in reactions to Falseta Virus, online audiences apply this concept to a highly diverse set of rhythmic practices.

The cultivation of technical skill alluded to earlier is not only a requirement for guitarists seeking opportunities for employment but also, as I will argue here, a powerful cultural framework that shapes contemporary identifications with the flamenco guitar. Virtuosity can be seen as a cultural framework since, apart from corresponding with musical complexity and skill, it also shapes the way that musical identities and communities are formed. Arguably, the artist who has most contributed to this framework is Paco de Lucía, who set entirely new technical and compositional standards for the flamenco guitar. Today, many aspiring flamenco guitarists, especially (though not exclusively) outside of Spain, establish their first contact with flamenco by browsing through online videos of Paco de Lucía and later generations of virtuosic guitarists, such as Tomatito and Vicente Amigo. In a way, the great technical skills of these artists have become a key factor of attraction for international audiences. This is exemplified by the fact that, today, many young flamenco guitarists from across the globe wield a superb technique and vast amounts of rhythmic and harmonic knowledge. Indeed, in the context of Falseta Virus it is evident that many contributors display levels of technical and musical knowledge that surpass by far those of Diego del Gastor. Another factor to consider here is that guitarists outside of Spain do not always have a choice but to start learning flamenco through disciplined solo practice before acquainting themselves with the accompaniment of song and dance, or with other forms of flamenco sociality.

The cultivation of technique, speed, and rhythmic complexity in flamenco guitar has been further accelerated, I argue, by the advent of digital media. In recent years, YouTube has become an important repository not only for recordings and live performances of flamenco guitar, such as those distributed by Solera Flamenca, but also for an ever-growing variety of pedagogical material. Apart from the videos and workshops alluded to in earlier sections, the platform houses a wealth of other 'how-to' videos with technical exercises for flamenco guitar. Many of such resources focus on picado, which is perhaps the most difficult right-hand technique that, not coincidentally, was brought to unmatched levels of speed and complexity by Paco de Lucía. For the development of rhythmic skill, more-over, students can now take advantage of a large number of online backing tracks and digital metronomes specifically made for flamenco, such as Flamenco Compás and Doctor Compás. Such tools offer well-organised collections of rhythmic support for almost all relevant flamenco styles, including different types of palmas, percussion, and even jaleos. Almost all guitarists whose work I have analysed in this section have utilised such backing tracks in their recordings.

While concepts of virtuosity have not yet been examined in detail for flamenco, scholarship on other guitar cultures, such as metal and rock, has demonstrated that musical virtuosity reflects wider conceptions of masculinity, heroism, and individualistic self-expression (Waksman, 2001; Walser, 1993). Discourses about the flamenco guitar and the reality of the flamenco guitar industry are underpinned by similar concepts of gender. For instance, female guitarists are still underrepresented in public performances of flamenco guitar (Chuse, 2015); sometimes they are even questioned for their alleged lack of strength and rhythmic feel.[62] While online tools for independent guitar practice do not inherently reproduce forms of gender inequality, arguably, they do stimulate perceptions of guitar practice in terms of strength, duress, and indi-vidualism – in other words, musical practice perceived as what Tia DeNora (1999) calls a 'technology of the self'. Thus, as the advent of virtuosity has propelled the flamenco guitar on a voyage towards ever-evolving forms of musical complexity and institutional recognition, it remains to be seen to what extent guitarists with other gender identities will be allowed to participate equally in that journey.

In previous pages, I have used Falseta Virus as a case study to explore how modern flamenco guitarists negotiate musical heritage in creative ways. Through their elaborations of the Zarzamora lick, a well-known composition that activates broader associations with locality, tradition, but also with border-crossing, the participants brought about a variety of identifications with the figure of Diego del Gastor, with the city of Morón, as well as with other places, traditions, and

---

[62] Some of these issues are discussed in an online interview between journalist Pablo San Nicasio and flamenco guitarist Antonia Jiménez: www.youtube.com/watch?v=CHtQzri3HJY.

identities. On a musical level, I have identified the coexistence of a variety of rhythmic practices in the submissions of various professional and non-professional guitarists, thus illustrating how these musicians negotiate the rhythmic heritage associated with Diego del Gastor and the city of Morón in ways that are complex and not always clearly identifiable. I have also explored how the diversity of rhythmic practices in Falseta Virus can be related to a variety of factors, such as new professional demands, the emergence of new cultural imaginaries around virtuosity, and the impact of digital tools on instrumental practice and performance. Curiously, despite these new realities, some viewers still detect traces of a local or traditional air in forms of playing that are rhythmically diverse and technically virtuosic. This suggests that perceptions of rhythmic feel and locality, even if not anchored in tangible musical realities, maintain an important role in contemporary flamenco discourse.

In the context of Falseta Virus, a friendly initiative launched to support musicians during Covid-19, this tension between rhythmic discourses and practices has virtually no broader consequences. However, when thinking about the ways in which flamenco participates in broader struggles over cultural heritage and belonging, perhaps there is a need to rethink such discursive identifications more critically. As we saw, rhythmic feel is a contested category whose perception, in some scenarios, continues to activate a variety of cultural, ethnic, and gendered stereotypes. To an extent, then, perceptions of rhythmic feel are dependent on assumptions about in-groups and out-groups – those who have it and those who don't – that cannot account for the complex realities and positionalities that shape flamenco guitar playing today. How might it be possible to overcome those stereotypes and enable ways of appreciating rhythmic feel across persistent borders? How, furthermore, can transnational rhythmic imaginaries coexist with the localised knowledges and inheritances that have shaped flamenco historically? Building on Falseta Virus, rhythmic feel reveals itself not only as a complex musical quality but also, to a large extent, as an aspiration, depending on our capability of detecting it in the performances and bodies of a broad variety of guitarists. Having rhythm, or *tener soniquete*, to evoke the lyrics of Paco de Lucía's composition that I began this Element with does not only depend on the guitarist but also on their audiences.

6 Conclusions

This Element has examined the intersections between rhythm and heritage in modern flamenco guitar. I have explored in what ways, and under what conditions, rhythm is practised, experienced, and transmitted as a distinctive type of cultural heritage, both in performances, discourses, and pedagogies of the instrument. I have posed these questions in response to a long intellectual tradition that considers rhythm as a musical skill that distinguishes some cultures and races from others. This tradition is perhaps most clearly reflected by the notion of the syncope, which points, on a musical level, to forms of irregular timing and accentual displacement, and on a broader cultural level, to the way that the rhythmic virtuosity of subjugated cultures might encode broader forms of disobedience and resistance.

Broadly speaking, this study has aimed to critically assess in what ways rhythm can be understood as heritage both from within and across cultural borders. I have done so by conceptualising heritage as an active form of identification with the past that can be established both on the level of musical discourse and practice. I have also explored how the motives and positionalities that shape identifications of rhythm as a shared inheritance are historically and contextually specific. On a discursive level, while perceptions of rhythmic feel as being culturally specific may seem anachronistic, they also reflect ongoing struggles over the ways in which localised musical cultures can best be supported by transnational heritage institutions and agendas. On a musical level, rhythm has the potential to facilitate but also to resist such cultural identifications with pre-existing localities, identities, and lineages. On the one hand, the communicative force of rhythm emanates from its ability to play with sedimented frameworks of meaning, such as the metrical structures and common accentuation patterns in flamenco guitar playing. On the other, rhythm's radical open-endedness also indicates that musical practice, to an extent, overflows its inscriptions into pre-available discourses and agendas. Ultimately, then, rhythm and heritage are similar in that they both emerge out of sedimented practices as well as gesturing towards new and open-ended identifications.

This Element has focused on perceptions and practices of rhythm not within institutionalised discourses and agendas, which have already received sustained critical attention in flamenco, but rather at a grassroots level. It is at this informal level where tactical (rather than strategic) identifications with heritage are performed in complex ways, thus giving insight into the artistic, cultural, and commercial negotiations of musical heritage by performers, pedagogues, and students. Specifically, I have explored how concepts of rhythmic skill and feel are mapped onto broader questions regarding cultural ownership, the protection and preservation of artistic knowledge, and localised forms of memory and heritage. As shown in Sections 3 and 4, distinctive forms of rhythmic playing in the cities of Jerez and Morón are often understood as performances of a shared local heritage. Here, I have explored how the pedagogical discourses of Diego del Morao and Dani del Morón, two recent exponents of the local guitar traditions in Jerez and Morón, point to the ways that the material realities of rhythmic practice – as reflected by their complex explorations of technique, timbre, and accentuation – overflow traditional concepts of local heritage. Both guitarists, then, hint at other possible places and trajectories with which such rhythmic forms of playing can be identified. Today, the association of rhythm with local lineages and traditions is taking new shapes and is being articulated across new cultural – and increasingly digital – routes. In Section 5, then, I have examined the case study of Falseta Virus, a guitar competition that was shaped by the social restrictions of the Covid-19 pandemic. This online initiative gives insight into the contemporary dynamics of rhythmic guitar playing, as well as into the multifarious ways in which the connections between rhythm and heritage are currently established.

Indeed, as reactions to Falseta Virus draw on elusive concepts of feel, air, and place, they raise broader questions about the ways in which musical lineages and inheritances are negotiated in increasingly decentred and transnational contexts of musical performance and pedagogy. Some of the scholarships on the Afro-diasporic lineages of rhythm with which I have dialogued in this Element, whilst offering powerful tools to explore the performative aspects of heritage, often remain dependent on the notion that the legacy and cultural memory of the African diaspora are somehow available, present, and stored in the (Black) body. To be sure, a similar concept of 'availability' exists in scholarship on the Spanish Roma and their intergenerational ways of transmitting flamenco. As already mentioned, it has not been my intention, nor do I consider it to be my place, to subdue the conception that the meanings of rhythm can be culturally specific. Nevertheless, it is worth interrogating the extent to which cultural memories and inheritances are a given; as well as the complex ways in which they may be acted upon by groups and individuals in the present.

Such criticisms about the complex acts and processes that shape understandings of heritage have already been articulated at an institutional level, such as in critiques about the heritage discourses and agendas of Andalusia's regional government (Venegas, 2017) and of global heritage agendas more broadly (Periáñez, 2019). In my view, such critiques need to be extended towards the heritage discourses and practices that circulate in non-institutional contexts of musical performance and pedagogy and to their various tactical functions in those spaces. On those levels, as well, the availability of ancestral lineages and the rootedness of musical knowledge in the body of the performer are far from a given reality. As Michael Rothberg notes in his discussion of the complex legacies of slavery, the process of inheritance across generations is often far from smooth and legacies can be highly contested, both in the family sphere and in society at large (2019, 64). In the context of flamenco, questions about the ethnic legacies that have shaped this music have traditionally also been a highly disputed issue. Anyone who engages with flamenco will have to navigate and evaluate not only the historical accuracy of claims about flamenco's historical roots but also, as Lou Charnon-Deutsch has observed, the great 'passion' of those who claim authority to speak on this issue (2004, 204). The pedagogical impacts of such questions should not be underestimated. As flamenco dancer and scholar Fernando López Rodríguez has asked, to what extent might claims about the transmission of flamenco between members of an in-group (such as the family sphere) erect pedagogical barriers for students that have not had access to such spaces (2020, 320–321)? How, furthermore, can the agency of such historical in-groups be restored and extended in such ways that it may also contribute to the journeys of musical learning of those who may be new to flamenco, but whose engagement with this music is equally embedded within complex cultural lineages and inheritances?

In this context, musical pedagogy and critical discourse have a potential to contribute radical and open-ended explorations of identity and heritage – especially when carried out across physical and cultural borders. For instance, the British-born and Seville-based flamenco dancer Yinka Esi Graves has noted how dance workshops with international students afford opportunities to rethink the cultural lineages and rhythms that flamenco shares with various Afro-diasporic dance styles and can thus help establish a 'common ground' with dancers familiar with those traditions.[63] In Sections 3 and 4, I have examined two online guitar workshops delivered by Diego del Morao and Dani de Morón and shown how their poetics and pedagogies of the flamenco guitar resist, if in subtle ways, common inscriptions of their music into pre-available lineages and traditions. The inchoate character of their respective critiques is symptomatic, I believe, of a dearth of pedagogical spaces where the broader cultural implications of flamenco guitar practice can be systematically explored. I hope that the present study has contributed an analytical framework that may help shape such spaces in the future.

The exact form that such pedagogical spaces may take will be impacted to a large extent by ongoing developments in the ever-intensifying global mediasphere. The technical and formal constraints, algorithms, and corporate interests of dominant information platforms are already having a crucial impact on the present outlook of flamenco performances and pedagogies and may do so to an even larger degree in the future. With this statement, I do not mean to reproduce common binaries about the sweeping potentials or profound risks of digital technologies (Tan, 2019). Rather, based on earlier examples I have provided, it

---

[63] Yinka Esi Graves discusses this issue at 12:05 in the following interview: www.youtube.com/watch?v=mqE-mhPbMvc.

is worth noting that certain impositions on, for instance, the accepted duration of a video, can have a relevant impact on the potentials of pedagogical material shared online to engage in a meaningful manner with concepts of musical heritage and transmission. In future years, as musicians across the globe will continue to renew the 'syntax, accent, and grammar' of flamenco (Cruces, 2015, 211), there is ample space for further critical work on the ways that different cultural identifications with this music are negotiated across online and offline contexts.

References

Abel, M. (2014). *Groove: An Aesthetics of Measured Time*. Leiden: Brill.

Agawu, K. (1995). The Invention of 'African' Rhythm. *Journal of the American Musicological Society*, **48(3)**, 380–395.

Agawu, K. (2016). The Rhythmic Imagination. In *The African Imagination in Music*. Oxford: Oxford University Press, pp. 155–194.

Agamennone, M., D. Palma, & G. Sarno, eds. (2022). *Sounds of the Pandemic: Accounts, Experiences, Perspectives in Times of COVID-19*. New York: Routledge.

Aix Gracia, F. (2014). *Flamenco y poder: un estudio desde la sociología del arte*. Madrid: Fundación SGAE.

Alivizatou, M. (2012). The Paradoxes of Intangible Heritage. In M. Stefano, P. Davis, & G. Corsane, eds., *Safeguarding Intangible Cultural Heritage*. Woodbridge: Boydell Press, pp. 9–21.

Álvarez Caballero, Á. (2003). *El toque flamenco*. Madrid: Alianza.

Andrade, M. d. (1972). *Ensaio sôbre a música brasileira*. São Paolo: Livraria Martins Editora.

Balfour, S. (2000). The Desarrollo Years, 1955–1975. In J. Álvarez-Junco & A. Shubert, eds., *A History of Spain since 1808*. London: Hodder Arnold, pp. 277–288.

Barletta, V. (2020). *Rhythm: Form and Dispossession*. Chicago: University of Chicago Press.

Berliner, P. (1994). *Thinking in Jazz: The Infinite Art of Improvisation*. Chicago: The University of Chicago Press.

Bethencourt Llobet, F. (2011). *Rethinking Tradition: Towards an Ethnomusicology of Contemporary Flamenco Guitar*. Newcastle University, unpublished PhD thesis.

Bonus, A. E. (2021). Maelzel, the Metronome, and the Modern Mechanics of Musical Time. In: M. Doffman, E. Payne & T. Young, eds., *The Oxford Handbook of Time in Music*. Oxford: Oxford University Press, pp. 303–340.

Brown, J. (2014). *Flamenco Capital: Tradition, Revolution and Renewal in Seville, Spain*. University of California, Riverside, unpublished PhD thesis.

Budasz, R. (2007). Black Guitar-Players and Early African-Iberian Music in Portugal and Brazil. *Early Music*, **35(1)**, 3–22.

Butterfield, M. (2006). The Power of Anacrusis: Engendered Feeling in Groove-Based Musics. *MTO: A Journal of the Society for Music Theory*, **12(4)**, 1–17.

Butterfield, M. (2010). Race and Rhythm: The Social Component of Swing Groove. *Jazz Perspectives*, **4(3)**, **301–335**. https://doi.org/10.1080/17494060.2010.561089.

Castaño, J. M. (2005). *De Jerez y sus cantes*. Córdoba: Almuzara.

Castro, G. (2015). El término 'bulería' en el flamenco. *Sinfonía Virtual*, **29**, **1–16**.

Castro, G. (2020). Músicas 'negras' y flamenco: relaciones musicales y traspasos entre músicas africanas, indígenas y españolas. *Sinfonía Virtual*, **39**, **1–147**.

Certeau, M. d. (1984). *The Practice of Everyday Life*. Los Angeles: University of California Press.

Charnon-Deutsch, L. (2004). *The Spanish Gypsy: The History of a Spanish Obsession*. University Park: Pennsylvania State University Press.

Chinoy, C. (2022). Flamenco Is Gitano: Reflections on the Expression of Gitano Identity in the Flamenco Fiesta. In K. M. Goldberg & A. Pizà, eds., *Celebrating Flamenco's Tangled Roots: The Body Questions*. Newcastle upon Tyne: Cambridge Scholars, pp. 321–342.

Chuse, L. (2015). Las Tocaoras: Women Guitarists and Their Struggle for Inclusion on the Flamenco Stage. In. K. M. Goldberg, N. Bennahum, & M. Heffner Hayes, eds., *Flamenco on the Global Stage: Historical, Critical and Theoretical Perspectives*. Jefferson: McFarland & Company, pp. 225–233.

Cohen, S., Roberts, L., Knifton, R., & Leonard, M. (2015). Introduction: Locating Popular Music Heritage. In S. Cohen, R. Knifton, M. Leonard & L. Roberts, eds., *Sites of Popular Music Heritage: Memories, Histories, Places*. New York: Routledge, pp. 1–11.

Crouch, D. (2015). Affect, Heritage, Feeling. In E. Waterton & S. Watson, eds., *The Palgrave Handbook of Contemporary Heritage Research*. London: Palgrave Macmillan, pp. 177–190.

Cruces Roldán, C. (2015). Normative Aesthetics and Cultural Constructions in Flamenco Dance: Female and Gitano Bodies as Legitimizers of Tradition. In K. M. Goldberg, N. Bennahum, & M. Heffner Hayes, eds., *Flamenco on the Global Stage: Historical, Critical and Theoretical Perspectives*. Jefferson: McFarland, pp. 210–224.

Cruces Roldán, C. (2023). Flamenco Heritage and the Politics of Identity. In M. Machin-Autenrieth, S. El-Shawan Castelo-Branco, & S. Llano, eds., *Music and the Making of Portugal and Spain*. Urbana: University of Illinois Press, pp. 267–285.

Crumbaugh, J. (2009). *Destination Dictatorship: The Spectacle of Spain's Tourism Boom and the Reinvention of Difference*. Albany: State University of New York Press.

Dawe, K. & M. Dawe. (2001). Handmade in Spain: The Culture of Guitar Making. In A. Bennett & K. Dawe, eds., *Guitar Cultures*. London: Routledge, pp. 63–87.

De Haro De San Mateo, M. V. & G. Marvin. (2015). The Bullfight in Twenty-First Century Spain: Polemics of Culture, Art and Ethics. In K. Nagai, K. Jones, & D. Landry et al, eds., *Cosmopolitan Animals*. Basingstoke: Palgrave Macmillan, pp. 93–106.

De la Torre, S. (2019). *El baile flamenco: un instrumento en los pies. Principios musicales de la percusión surgidos de la danza*. Universidad Complutense de Madrid, unpublished PhD thesis.

Denning, M. (2015). *Noise Uprising: The Audiopolitics of a World Musical Revolution*. London: Verso.

DeNora, T. (1999). Music as a Technology of the Self. *Poetics*, **27(1)**, **31–56**.

Didi-Huberman, G. (2008). *El bailaor de soledades*, translated by Dolores Aguilera. Valencia: Pre-Textos.

Diouf, M. & I. Kiddoe Nwankwo. (2010a). Introduction. In M. Diouf & I. Kiddoe Nwankwo, eds., *Rhythms of the Afro-Atlantic World: Rituals and Remembrances*. Ann Arbour: University of Michigan Press, pp. 1–16.

Diouf, M. & I. Kiddoe Nwankwo, eds. (2010b). *Rhythms of the Afro-Atlantic World: Rituals and Remembrances*. Ann Arbour: University of Michigan Press.

Faucher, A. (1996). *Flamenco: Morao y Oro: Moraíto (transcripción de seis toques)*. Paris: Affedis.

Feldman, H. C. (2006). *Black Rhythms of Peru: Reviving African Musical Heritage in the Black Pacific*. Connecticut: Wesleyan University Press.

Foster, S. L. (2010). Muscle/Memories: How Germaine Acogny and Diane McIntyre Put Their Feet Down. In M. Diouf & I. Kiddoe Nwankwo, eds., *Rhythms of the Afro-Atlantic World: Rituals and Remembrances*. Ann Arbour: University of Michigan Press, pp. 121–135.

Galle Baggenstoss, J. (2022). The New Flamenco School Show: Breaking Stereotypes and Planting Seeds of Discourse on Race. In K. M. Goldberg & A. Pizà, eds., *Celebrating Flamenco's Tangled Roots: The Body Questions*. Newcastle upon Tyne: Cambridge Scholars, pp. 430–437.

Gamboa, J. M. & F. Núñez. (2007). *Flamenco de la A a la Z: Diccionario de términos del flamenco*. Barcelona: Espasa.

Goldberg, K. M. (2014). Sonidos Negros: On the Blackness of Flamenco. *Dance Chronicle*, **37(1)**, **85–113**.

Goldberg, K. M. (2019). *Sonidos Negros: On the Blackness of Flamenco*. New York: Oxford University Press.

Goldberg, K. M., N. Bennahum, & M. Heffner Hayes, eds. (2015). *Flamenco on the Global Stage: Historical, Critical and Theoretical Perspectives*. Jefferson: McFarland.

González, A. (2021). *Paseando por la Granada flamenca: Paisajes sonoros de la guitarra*. Granada: Diputación de Granada.

Granados, M. (2004). *Armonía del flamenco: aplicado a la guitarra flamenca*. Barcelona: Publicacions Beethoven.

Gray, L. E. (2013). *Fado Resounding: Affective Politics and Urban Life*. Durham: Duke University Press.

Harrar, E. (n.d.). Rhythm lesson: bulerías, soleares & alegrías. http://gypsyfla menco.com/flamenco%20ordering.html.

Harrison, R. (2012). *Heritage: Critical Approaches*. New York: Routledge.

Hesmondhalgh, D., R. Campos Valverde, D. Bondy Valdovinos Kaye, & Z. Li. (2023). The Impact of algorithmically driven recommendation systems on music consumption and production – A literature review. www.gov.uk/gov ernment/publications/research-into-the-impact-of-streaming-services-algo rithms-on-music-consumption/the-impact-of-algorithmically-driven-recom mendation-systems-on-music-consumption-and-production-a-literature-review.

Jiménez de Cisneros, B. (2015). *Ritmo y compás: análisis musical del flamenco*. Barcelona: Atril Flamenco.

Jiménez de Cisneros, B. (2020). *Las palmas flamencas: Aproximación musicológica a través de la fonografía y la práxis contemporánea*. Barcelona: Atril Flamenco.

Kirshenblatt-Gimblett, B. (1995). Theorizing Heritage. *Ethnomusicology*, **39 (3), 367–380**.

Kliman, N. P. (2020a). Compás explained. www.canteytoque.es.

Kliman, N. P. (2020b). Morón-Jerez. www.canteytoque.es.

Kliman, N. P. (2020c). A falseta recorded by old and modern guitarists. www .canteytoque.es.

Kliman, N. P. (2023). A study of the alzapúa technique. www.canteytoque.es.

Lerdahl, F. & R. Jackendoff. (1983). *A Generative Theory of Tonal Music*. Cambridge, MA: MIT Press.

Lie, S. B. (2017). The Politics of 'Understanding': Secrecy, Language, and Manouche Song. *Ethnic and Racial Studies*, **40(1), 96–113**.

Loiacono, V. & J. Fallon. (2018). Intangible Cultural Heritage beyond Borders: Egyptian Bellydance (Raqs Sharqi) as a Form of Transcultural Heritage. *Journal of Intercultural Studies*, **39(3), 286–304**.

López Rodríguez, F. (2020). *Historia queer del flamenco: desvíos, transiciones y retornos en el baile flamenco (1808–2018)*. Barcelona: Egales.

Machin-Autenrieth, M. (2017). *Flamenco, Regionalism and Musical Heritage in Southern Spain*. London: Routledge.

Mairena, A. & R. Molina. (1963). *Mundo y formas del cante flamenco*. Madrid: Revista de Occidente.

Manuel, P. (2006). Flamenco in Focus: An Analysis of a Performance of Soleares. In M. Tenzer, ed., *Analytical Studies in World Music*. Oxford: Oxford University Press, pp. 92–119. https://doi.org/10.1093/acprof:oso/9780195177893.003.0004.

Manuel, P. (2010). Composition, Authorship, and Ownership in Flamenco, Past and Present. *Ethnomusicology*, **54(1)**, 106–135.

Márquez, N. (2022). Dancing My Otherness/Multiplicity or *Sin Pedir Permiso, Me Agarro Aquí*. In K. M. Goldberg & A. Pizà, eds., *Celebrating Flamenco's Tangled Roots: The Body Questions*. Newcastle upon Tyne: Cambridge Scholars, pp. 296–313.

McDowell, J. H. (2015). 'Surfing the Tube' for Latin American Song: The Blessings (and Curses) of YouTube. *Journal of American Folklore*, **128(509)**, **260–272**.

Meyer, L. (1956). *Emotion and Meaning in Music*. Chicago: University of Chicago Press.

Mitchell, T. (1994). *Flamenco Deep Song*. New Haven: Yale University Press.

Núñez, F. (2021). *América en el flamenco*. Madrid: Flamencópolis.

Ochoa, A. M. (2003). *Músicas locales en tiempos de globalización*. Buenos Aires: Norma.

Ordóñez Eslava, P. (2020). *Apología de lo impuro: Contramemoria y f[r]icción en el Flamenco contemporáneo*. Ciudad Real: CIOFF España.

Periáñez, I. (2016). Ser y sentir flamenco: descolonizando la estética moderno colonial desde los bordes. *Revista andaluza de antropología*, **10**, 29–53. http://dx.doi.org/10.12795/RAA.2016.10.03.

Periáñez, I. (2019). Discursos y representaciones locales sobre la patrimonialización del flamenco en Andalucía, un proceso multinivel. *Revista de Antropología Social*, **28(1)**, 71–93.

Periáñez, I. (2023). *Cosmosonoridades: Cante-gitano y canción-gyu: Epistemologías del sentir*. Madrid: Akal.

Pryer, A. (2019). Musical Heritage as a Global and Cultural Concept. In B. Norton & N. Matsumoto, eds., *Music as Heritage: Historical and Ethnographic Perspectives*. London: Routledge, pp. 21–41.

Radano, R. (2003). *Lying Up a Nation: Race and Black Music*. Chicago: University of Chicago Press.

Ramos, J. (2010). Descarga acústica. *Papel Máquina: Revista de cultura*, **2(4)**, **49–77**.

Rina, C. (2017). El jardin de los senderos que se bifurcan: Diego del Gastor, Donn Pohren y el canon flamenco. Unpublished document, pp. 1–35.

Rioja, E. (1995a). La pretendida 'incorporación' de la guitarra al cante. In J. L. Navarro García & M. Ropero Núñez, eds., *Historia del flamenco*. Vol. II. Sevilla: Ediciones Tartessos, pp. 11–21.

Rioja, E. (1995b). El acompañamiento guitarrístico en los primeros tiempos del flamenco: Sus técnicas. In J. L. Navarro García & M. Ropero Núñez, eds., *Historia del flamenco*. Vol. II. Sevilla: Ediciones Tartessos, pp. 25–33.

Rioja, E. (1995c). Francisco Díaz Fernández 'Paco de Lucena'. In J. L. Navarro García & M. Ropero Núñez, eds., *Historia del flamenco*. Vol. II. Sevilla: Ediciones Tartessos, pp. 151–157.

Rioja, E. (1995d). Las escuelas de toque. In J. L. Navarro García & M. Ropero Núñez, eds., *Historia del flamenco*. Vol. II. Sevilla: Ediciones Tartessos, pp. 159–163.

Rioja, E. (1995e). Julián Arcas. In J. L. Navarro García & M. Ropero Núñez, eds., *Historia del flamenco*. Vol. II. Sevilla: Ediciones Tartessos, pp. 165–171.

Rioja, E. (2003). El llamado *toque de Morón*: ¿Una escuela guitarrística? Unpublished document, pp. 1–25. www.jondoweb.com/contenido-el-toque-de-moron-748.html.

Robbins, D. (2015). Polyrhythm and the Valorization of Time in Three Movements. *Brasiliana: Journal for Brazilian Studies*, **4(1)**, 82–109.

Rodríguez, R. (2014). *Razón de son*. Madrid: Fol Música.

Romero Naranjo, F. (2008). Percusión corporal en diferentes culturas. *Música y Educación*, **21(76)**, 46–96.

Rothberg, M. (2019). *The Implicated Subject: Beyond Victims and Perpetrators*. Stanford: Stanford University Press.

Said, E. (1978). *Orientalism*. New York: Vintage Books.

Sainz, J. & M. Mbengue. (2022). *En clave flamenca: Otras perspectivas en el tratamiento del lenguaje rítmico flamenco y su aplicación a la percusión*. Q-book, Cultura Integral.

Sanlúcar, M. (2005). *Sobre la guitarra flamenca: Teoría y Sistema para la Guitarra Flamenca*. Córdoba: Ayuntamiento de Córdoba.

Sauvanet, P. (2000). *Le rythme et la raison: 1 – Rythmologiques*. Paris: Éditions Kimé.

Scruton, R. (1997). *The Aesthetics of Music*. Oxford: Oxford University Press.

Seisdedos, I. (2017). Diego Carrasco: 'Con el tiempo aprenderé a cantar'. *El País, Babelia*, 18 November.

Sody de Rivas, Á. (2004). *Diego del Gastor: El eco de unos toques*. Madrid: El Flamenco Vive.

Suárez Japón, J. M. (2014). *Sinelo Calorró: Conversaciones con Manuel Morao*. Cádiz: Diputación de Cádiz.

Tan, S. E. (2019). Digital Inequalities and Global Sounds. In N. Cook, M. Ingalls, & D. Trippett, eds., *The Cambridge Companion to Music in Digital Culture*. Cambridge: Cambridge University Press, pp. 253–273. https://doi.org/10.1017/9781316676639.025.

Tan, S. E. (2021). Whose Decolonisation? Checking for Intersectionality, Lane-Policing and Academic Privilege from a Transnational (Chinese) Vantage Point. *Ethnomusicology Forum*, **30(1)**, **140–162**.

Taylor, D. (2003). *The Archive and the Repertoire: Performing Cultural Memory in the Americas*. Durham: Duke University Press.

Torres Cortés, N. (2012). La tradición oral en el toque flamenco: recordando a Moraíto Chico. *La Madrugá: Revista de investigación sobre el flamenco*, **7**, **55–77**.

Torres Cortés, N. (2020). El concepto de toque flamenco. *La Madrugá, revista de investigación sobre el flamenco*, **17**, **136–165**.

Vázquez García, P. L. (2016). *La época dorada del Flamenco en Morón de la Frontera (1960–1970)*. Sevilla: Diputación de Sevilla.

Vega, J. B. (1995). El maestro Patiño. In J. L. Navarro García & M. Ropero Núñez, eds., *Historia del flamenco*. Vol. II. Sevilla: Ediciones Tartessos, pp. 143–145.

Venegas, J. L. (2017). Populism without the People: The Cultural Politics of the Junta de Andalucía. *Arizona Journal of Hispanic Cultural Studies*, **21**, **215–233**.

Vital, L. (2020). La escuela jerezana del toque. https://lauravital.es/la-escuela-jerezana-del-toque.

Waksman, S. (2001). Into the Arena: Edward Van Halen and the Cultural Contradictions of the Guitar Hero. In A. Bennett & K. Dawe, eds., *Guitar Cultures*. London: Routledge, pp. 117–134.

Walser, R. (1993). *Running with the Devil: Power, Gender, and Madness in Heavy Metal Music*. Hanover: Wesleyan University Press.

Washabaugh, W. (2012). *Flamenco Music and National Identity in Spain*. Surrey: Ashgate.

Waterton, E. & S. Watson. (2015). Heritage as a Focus of Research: Past, Present and New Directions. In E. Waterton & S. Watson, eds., *The Palgrave Handbook of Contemporary Heritage Research*. London: Palgrave Macmillan, pp. 1–17.

Witek, M. (2016). Filling In: Syncopation, Pleasure, and Distributed Embodiment in Groove. *Music Analysis*, **36(1)**, **138–160**. https://doi.org/10.1111/musa.12082.

Woods Peiró, E. (2012). *White Gypsies: Race and Stardom in Spanish Musicals*. Minneapolis: University of Minnesota Press.

Worms, C. (2011). *Guitares flamenca de Jerez* (2 vols.). Le Vallier: Delatour.

Zuckerkandl, V. (1959). *The Sense of Music*. Princeton: Princeton University Press.

Acknowledgements

I would like to express my gratitude to Simon Blackmore for his generous and invaluable help in creating the musical transcriptions for this Element, and to Víctor Morata García for his helpful suggestions about aspects of music theory. I also wish to thank the series editor and anonymous reviewers for their helpful and detailed feedback about an earlier version of the manuscript.

Cambridge Elements ≡

Music Since 1945

Mervyn Cooke
University of Nottingham

Mervyn Cooke brings to the role of series editor an unusually broad range of expertise, having published widely in the fields of twentieth-century opera, concert and theatre music, jazz, and film music. He has edited and co-edited *Cambridge Companions to Britten, Jazz, Twentieth-Century Opera*, and *Film Music*. His other books include *Britten: War Requiem, Britten and the Far East, A History of Film Music, The Hollywood Film Music Reader, Pat Metheny: The ECM Years*, and two illustrated histories of jazz. He is currently co-editing (with Christopher R. Wilson) *The Oxford Handbook of Shakespeare and Music*.

About the Series

Elements in Music Since 1945 is a highly stimulating collection of authoritative online essays that reflects the latest research into a wide range of musical topics of international significance since the Second World War. Individual Elements are organised into constantly evolving clusters devoted to such topics as art music, jazz, music and image, stage and screen genres, music and media, music and place, immersive music, music and movement, music and politics, music and conflict, and music and society. The latest research questions in theory, criticism, musicology, composition and performance are also given cutting-edge and thought-provoking coverage. The digital-first format allows authors to respond rapidly to new research trends, with contributions being updated to reflect the latest thinking in their fields, and the essays are enhanced by the provision of an exciting range of online resources.

Cambridge Elements ⁼

Music Since 1945

Elements in the Series

Printed in the United States
by Baker & Taylor Publisher Services